I0412791

URGENT CALL

THE IMPERATIVE FOR REGIME CHANGE AND SOCIETAL TRANSFORMATION IN

RWANDA

Selected Writings

Dr. Theogene Rudasingwa

Tribute to the late Colonel Patrick Karegeya, a freedom fighter assassinated by agents of General Paul Kagame's fascist regime.

We must take sides. Neutrality helps the oppressor, never the victim. Silence encourages the tormentor, never the tormented. Sometimes we must interfere. When human lives are endangered, when human dignity is in jeopardy, national borders and sensitivities become irrelevant. Wherever men and women are persecuted because of their race, religion, or political views, that place must - at that moment - become the center of the universe.

— Elie Wiesel, *The Night Trilogy: Night/Dawn/The Accident*

TABLE OF CONTENTS

1

ABSOLUTE POWER AT ANY PRICE

Speech at the Colloque

Paris.

1st April 2014

Thank you Mr. President for inviting me to speak at this event.

I thank the organizers for their generosity and hospitality.

Let me also take this opportunity to thank the distinguished speakers and participants, gathered today to discuss a timely and yet very challenging subject: the Rwandan drama, and truth, as narrated by actors in this drama.

As we begin our deliberations, we are painfully reminded of the timing of this event. For all of us Rwandans, April is always a very difficult month. We both want to remember and forget it, for the pain it evokes is enduring and defining.

Twenty years later, we still remember the horror, when Rwandans killed Rwandans.

So let us keep silent for one minute to remember all those who perished during the genocide and massacres of 1994.

As you all know, Rwanda is a centuries old nation, famously known for its two ethnic groups, the Hutu and Tutsi. There is a third, Twa, always conveniently ignored by Rwandans and non-Rwandans because it has not been actively part of the recent Rwandan drama.

To understand how President Kagame and the ruling party, the Rwandese Patriotic Front (RPF), exercise absolute power, I would like to briefly mention three pivotal moments in Rwanda's history in the last 100 years, each of which bore the seeds that produced the succeeding series of events:

- Monarchical rule comes under German colonization at the end of the 19th century, succeeded by Belgian colonization until 1962.
- Rwanda becomes a Republic after the 1959 (Hutu) Revolution
- The Rwandese Patriotic Front (Tutsi) invasion of 1990 and its capture of state power in 1994

The pre-1959 period saw the rise of a marginalized Hutu population led by a Hutu elite that challenged the monarchist status quo. The birth of the Rwandan Republic, and the end of the Belgian colonialism, was a violent phenomenon. While bringing social, economic and political benefits to the previously marginalized Hutu community, the 1959 revolution ended up marginalizing the Tutsi community.

Many Tutsi were massacred, and hundreds of thousands fled into exile. The revolution produced Tutsi refugees, followed by waves of insurgency (INYENZI) that ended in the 1960s.

Within Rwanda, the short-lived multiparty politics abruptly ended, as the political space was closed and the country became a one-party state, under MDR PARMEHUTU party. Power also became over-centralized in the hands of President Gregoire Kayibanda, who with time, relied more and more on Hutu from his community in Gitarama, in southern Rwanda.

In 1973, there was a palace coup within the revolution, and General Juvenal Habyarimana, a Hutu from the north, came to power, subsequently forming his own party, MRND.
The regime remained a Hutu one, and increasingly biased in favor of the north. Rwanda was still a one-party state. Like the previous monarchy before 1959, and Kayibanda's regime until 1973, power became over-centralized in the hands of President Habyarimana.

Tutsi remained in exile, and marginalized within the country. Towards the end of the 1980s and beginning with 1990, President Habyarimana's regime had lost momentum and was under attack internally from political parties (mainly of Hutu from the south) and from an invasion by Tutsi refugees (RPF) from Uganda.

Under political, economic, military and diplomatic pressure, President Habyarimana reluctantly negotiated the Arusha Peace Agreement with RPF. The peace agreement provided a vision for democratization and the rule of law, power sharing among MRND, RPF and other opposition political parties, establishment of new security institutions (Army and Gendarmerie), and the return of the 1959 refugees.

For a brief moment, Rwandans were hopeful that peace, reconciliation, democracy and the rule of law were coming to Rwanda at last.

Then General Paul Kagame struck, ordering the shooting down of the plane in which President Habyarimana, the President of Burundi Cyprien Ntaryamira, French citizens, and all others on board were killed. This assassination triggered genocide and massacres. RPF finally captured state power in July 1994, by winning the civil war, and ending the Arusha Peace Agreement, as we know it.

As Rwanda commemorates 20 years of President Paul Kagame's reign of terror, it is important to identify the fundamental aspects of his strategy to keep himself and RPF in absolute, violent power.

First: because it was power obtained through violent means, by a minority, it has had to seek legitimacy through the construction of a narrative, a story line so to speak, that begins with genocide, continues with genocide, defines the raison d'etre of the regime and is projected into the future.

According to this narrative, Hutu extremists shot down President Habyarimana's plane to find cause to start genocide. Belgian colonization is the ideological parent of the ethnic divisions and genocidal ideology. The French helped the Hutu in committing genocide, and the international community abandoned Rwanda. Rwanda's recovery is phenomenal, and Rwandans owe it to RPF and its sole hero, President Paul Kagame. The RPF regime has even banned French as a language of instruction in Rwanda as part of this new narrative.

Every change must have its narrative and its disciples. And it must have friends to champion and protect it, and enemies against whom it must mobilize and organize. France and the Hutu were initially the only enemies.

The United States and the United Kingdom emerged as the new friends, while Tony Blair and President Clinton became the passionate champions of the new gospel. Anyone who does not agree with this narrative is considered a divisive revisionist and genocidaire.

Second: since coming to power in 1994, Kagame's RPF regime has used organized violence and war as instruments of domestic and foreign policy within and outside Rwanda: the shooting down of President Habyarimana's plane which triggered genocide; the murder of Rwandan bishops and priests (1994); the Robert Gersony Report that documented widespread massacres by RPF (1994); the Kibeho massacres (1995); the UN Mapping Report of 2010 that documented war crimes, crimes against humanity, and even possible acts of genocide against Hutu; assassinations of opponents in Rwanda and abroad, just to mention a few.

In 1994, it assassinated the President of Burundi, Cyprien Ntaryamira.

In 2001, it assassinated the President of the Democratic Republic of Congo, Laurent Kabila, having invaded that country twice and still maintaining its presence through proxies like M23. Close to 6 million Congolese people have perished due to Kagame's policies and actions in DRC.

Kagame's troops fought Ugandan troops in the DRC in 2000. He has picked fights with Tanzania and now South Africa. He has fought Zimbabwe, Angola and Namibia in the DRC.

Third: within the military and security institutions, he has created an army within an army (Republican Guard and Special Forces), competing intelligence services and informal networks, while retrenching or otherwise marginalizing any real or perceived competitors.

The military are the backbone of the Rwanda government. President Kagame discusses major policies and decisions with senior military commanders before discussing them with civilian assistants. Selected military commanders are the real government; the civilians in government are the technocratic servants of the military. The Rwanda Defense Forces are, in essence, not a national army. They owe allegiance not to the state, or its people, but to one political organization, the Rwandese Patriotic Front, and to its supreme leader, President Kagame. No wonder he calls RDF, "my army", and its officers, "my officers".

The RDF is spread throughout the country, and its officers deployed across the world in embassies and as agents in a vast global network. They perform many political functions on behalf of the RPF. The military are responsible for mobilization for the party.

They convince or coerce opinion leaders to join and serve the RPF.

Military officers are responsible for the supervision of the local government officials that the RPF appoints.

RDF is responsible for the rigging of elections in favor of the RPF, and military officers are responsible for ensuring that opponents of the regime everywhere are identified and destroyed.

RDF officers are almost 100% Tutsi!

Fourth: within the Rwandese Patriotic Front, his strategy is to marginalize or eliminate real or perceived enemies, and transform the party into a rubber stamp to enforce the will of the President.

The Rwandese Patriotic Front is unofficially the sole party that is allowed to practice politics in Rwanda.

The party is President's Kagame's tool for controlling every aspect of life in Rwanda. The party controls the country through the officials that it appoints to public office at all levels. Its members constitute the overwhelming majority of all institutions.

The party maintains strict control of all these officials by requiring them to take an oath and through disciplinary procedures that are a violation of the laws that require certain public officials to be independent.

The party secretariat functions as a parallel office of the Prime Minister. The RPF Secretariat is responsible for the appointment of all civilian public officials, including ministers, judges, and legislators; draws recommendations for Kagame to approve, if he has made his decision beforehand.

It is responsible for discussing and approving all policy development, including all policy proposals and major decisions to be discussed by Parliament; disciplining all civilian public officials who are members of the party, including ministers, judges, and legislators, who by law should be independent. The party is a vast network of informal government mechanisms that operate at all levels of the organization of state administration.

Fifth: formal Government institutions (Parliament, Judiciary and the Executive) are situated very far down the ladder in the power structure of Rwanda. Hutu who are accommodated by the system are mainly found in the formal government. Members of the formal government are merely technocrats implementing the policies of others and are not influential unless they happen to have strong connections in the party, the military, or with the President and his wife.

In fact, the RPF ensures that the most important government departments are delegated to very trusted Tutsi members.

Tutsi controls all the institutions that are most critical to President Kagame's strategies for maintaining absolute power. These include the Central Bank, Ministry of Finance, Ministry of Health, Rwanda Revenue Authority, Ministry of Justice and Ministry of Foreign Affairs.

Sixth: with regard to political parties, the strategy is to co-opt, corrupt, marginalize or destroy them. Since the short-lived experience of working with other political parties in 1995, RPF under President Paul Kagame has completely closed political space for political parties. The only political parties that are allowed to legally exist and function in Rwanda are those that are allied to RPF. Opposition leaders who have dared to exercise the right to participate in Rwandan politics independently are jailed, (former President Pasteur Bizimungu, Charles Ntakirutinka, Victoire Ingabire, Bernard Ntaganda, Deo Mushaidi, and others), killed, or end up in exile.

Seventh: closed space for independent media, civil society and free intellectual expression. Rwandan journalists, human rights activists and NGO leaders have been jailed, killed in and outside Rwanda, and independent newspapers banned.

Eighth: manipulate relationship with foreigners, using guilt and intimidation. President Kagame and RPF have cultivated an elaborate network of foreigners (and a few Rwandans) that have to sell President Kagame's image and narrative as the sole hero and savior of Rwanda.

Because Rwanda is heavily dependent on aid, and his reputation as the western-celebrated leader of the "emerging Singapore of Africa" is crucial to the continuous flow of aid, this group of people is crucial in facilitating him. Through what he calls the Presidential Advisory Council (PAC), he is able to promote a soft and deceptive image abroad, especially where it matters most, in the United States and the United Kingdom.

Through lobbying, public relations, and access to the media, these facilitators help President Kagame's self-promotion abroad, and shield him from accountability for the crimes he commits on Rwanda, DRC and abroad.

The loudest and most powerful in the whole group are Tony Blair, President Bill Clinton, and the American evangelist, Rick Warren. They market President Paul Kagame as one of the most visionary leaders in the world.

Ninth: through his personal and absolute control of money matters, President Kagame finances a three-pronged strategy for sustaining his control of power in Rwanda:

(a) Establishing intelligence systems that are able to identify and neutralize all real or perceived threats;

(b) Maintaining a strong military that is able both to protect the regime and to project his power abroad; and,

(c) Securing the resources to finance the activities of the military and security institutions that keep him in power.

For these resources, President Kagame draws both on public resources and on the business activities of the RPF. The men and women who are responsible for generating, managing and delivering these resources are very influential.

Crystal Ventures (formerly Tri-Star Investments) and the Horizon Group, the business enterprises that President Kagame owns, ostensibly belong to the RPF and the Defense Department, but are practically his personal businesses. He alone controls this business empire. The accounts of the businesses are secret and never audited independently. The managers of the businesses are answerable to Kagame alone. Kagame does not account to any organ of the RPF on these business and finance matters.

Tenth: the central and decisive piece in the contemporary Rwandan drama is President Kagame himself. I am often asked, "What motivates Paul Kagame? How has his character, shaped by being a refugee at a tender age, his involvement in violent wars in Uganda, Rwanda and DRC affected his outlook on life?"

Since the 1980s, Paul Kagame has been at the center of violent conflicts spanning the territories of Uganda, Rwanda and the Democratic Republic of Congo. In these conflicts, there has been widespread destruction of life and horrendous human rights abuses. Kagame bears personal as well as command responsibility for many of these crimes, including assassinations and other serious human rights violations.

After a lifetime of unimaginable violence, Kagame has become a serial killer and mass murderer. He is a person with no regrets or remorse for the acts of violence that he or others acting on his instructions commit. He is not apologetic about this. On the contrary, he makes it a point in public and private conversations that indeed his opponents must die.

About his recent victim, Colonel Patrick Karegeya, assassinated in Johannesburg, South Africa, President Kagame coldly said, " Rwanda did not kill this person…I wish Rwanda did it..I really wish it".

Asked about the shooting down of President Habyarimana's plane, he was quoted as saying, "I don't give a damn."

In addition, he is relentless, and always takes bigger risks, far beyond rational behavior. A few weeks after assassinating Col Karegeya, Rwandan agents tried to assassinate General Kayumba Nyamwasa for the third time, triggering a diplomatic crisis between South Africa and Rwanda.

Probably a result of his past crimes, President Kagame is very paranoid about plots to remove him from power and about his security in general.

Kagame's actions are influenced in large measure by a reckoning with his past. Kagame believes that a person's name or reputation is his or her most precious possession. He has established a false reputation of frugality, incorruptibility, accountability in government, and military hero who stopped the genocide. Preserving this false image is critical to the preservation of Kagame's monopoly of power in Rwanda.

Kagame's greatest concern is that of the people who have information (including corruption and responsibility for assassinations, war crimes and crimes against humanity, in Uganda, Rwanda and the DRC) which may tarnish the public image that he has created.

Kagame's criminal background, and the need to avoid being held accountable, explains why he is bent on staying in power at all costs, including the assassination of political opponents, especially those who know him very well.

Ladies and Gentlemen,

Let me summarize the salient features of President Paul Kagame's and RPF's 20 year reign of terror: a distorted and deceptive narrative that criminalizes Hutu in particular and all his opponents in general; over- reliance on violence and war-making nationally and regionally; "Tutsi-fication" of the leadership of the military while eliminating real and potential competitors; transformation of the ruling RPF into a rubber stamp to enforce his will while eliminating real or perceived contenders to power; usurping and over-centralization of legislative, executive and judiciary powers; closure of political space for political parties, civil society, independent media and intellectual activity; personal control of a financial empire that is spread across public and private sectors; and, a mindset of a serial killer and mass murderer who relentlessly acts with impunity.

It is this state of affairs that led some of us former members of RPF and partners of President Paul Kagame to break ranks and, with others Rwandans across the ethnic divide establish the Rwanda National Congress (RNC), with the following objectives:

- Stop and prevent violent conflict, including genocide and grave human rights violations that Rwanda's people have periodically suffered and that have historically extended to citizens – men, women, and children – of neighboring states;

- Eradicate a culture of impunity for human rights violations;

- Create a conducive and progressive environment for inclusive social and economic development for all the people of Rwanda;

- Establish, nurture and institutionalize democratic governance, particularly the rule of law in all its aspects;

- Establish independent, non-partisan, professional civil service and security institutions;

- Build a stable society that promotes and protects equality, embraces and celebrates diversity, and fosters inclusion in all aspects of national life;

- Promote individual, community and national reconciliation and healing;

- Promote harmonious relations, reconciliation and mutually- beneficial collaboration with the peoples and governments of neighboring states;

- Resolve the chronic problem of Rwandan refugees; and,

- Nurture a culture of tolerance to diverse ideas, freedom of discussion, and debate of critical issues.

At the heart of our program, widely shared with the majority of Rwandans and in the political platform our organization belongs to with FDU-Inkingi and AMAHORO Peoples Party, is the triple challenge to:

a) Build an army and security institutions that are national instead of being hostage to ethnic-based cliques;

b) Ensuring fundamental freedoms and democracy with guarantees for minorities;

c) Pursuing truth, reconciliation and justice for all as indispensable conditions for sustainable peace in Rwanda and the Great Lakes region.

We have preached this as the pathway to peaceful change but President Paul Kagame has responded consistently with violence, resolutely stating and acting to exclude any possibility for peaceful reforms in Rwanda.

Now Rwanda, as in 1959 and 1994, is at crossroads again, bending towards civil war and more bloodshed.

President Paul Kagame and his RPF are armed and dangerous and have taken 11 million Rwandans hostage, and threaten, once again, to put the whole Great Lakes region on fire.

Another civil war and genocide are not inevitable but preventable. However, the window of opportunity is closing fast.

The international community has an obligation to help Rwandans resist, contain, stop and reverse President Paul Kagame's reign of terror. Twenty years of appeasement have simply made his regime more intransigent and ever ready to act with impunity.

The first step in this process is to get the narrative on Rwanda right. I am glad this conference seeks to do that.

The second step is to overcome fear and guilt and speak out. History shows that fear and silence are very powerful weapons in the hands of dictatorial regimes.

The third step is to do no harm. If you cannot help Rwandan people, at least do not help those who are killing them. To those in alliance with him in London and Washington DC, we say to you, "enough is enough, stop aiding and rewarding President Kagame's criminal behavior."

Lastly, let us connect and network. Dictatorial regimes love to face the oppressed in isolation, and to vanquish them one by one.

If we can pool our minds and actions together, we will make France's motto, "Liberty, Equality, and Fraternity", itself a universal human aspiration, relevant and possible for Rwanda's future as it has been for the French for centuries now.

Thank you!

2

OPEN LETTER TO BENJAMIN NETANYAHU, PRIME MINISTER OF ISRAEL, THE JEWISH PEOPLE, AND ALL CITIZENS OF ISRAEL (*April, 2014*)

Today I have read with concern reports from Israel's Jerusalem Post and Haaretz that the Government of Israel is sending African asylum seekers to Rwanda. If this is true, these are troubling developments, especially coming at a time when there are equally troubling concerns that the Government of Israel in particular, and Jews in general, have become very close to the regime of President Paul Kagame.

You are aware as much as I of Israel's own history, and the plight of Jews over millennia, in exile across the world. I am aware as much as you are about the tribulations of the Jewish people, especially before, during, and after the Holocaust, and the challenges that the state of Israel has faced since its founding in 1948.

I am familiar with statelessness. I have been a refugee for most of my lifetime. I lost my own father and many of my kith and kin in the violent troubles that have beset Rwanda since 1959. I was witness to the 1994 Rwanda genocide, and the massacres that succeeded it. Having been a refugee in Burundi, Tanzania, Kenya and Uganda in the past, my latest location as a refugee is the United States. I have been fortunate to serve Rwanda in various capacities: Secretary General of Rwanda's ruling party, the Rwandese Patriotic Front; Rwanda's Ambassador to the United States; and President Paul Kagame's Chief of Staff. And like President Kagame, I am Tutsi.

As I read these stories of poor stateless Africans, I am outraged by the behavior of African rulers whose mistakes and omissions are fueling this massive hemorrhage from Africa, whose youth continue to die on high seas or become stateless.

I also wonder why, notwithstanding Israel's many other considerations regarding immigration, it would not welcome and accept as its own these strangers in your land. If on moral and humanitarian grounds you cannot shoulder this responsibility, at least you could proceed in a more open and transparent manner to dispose these seemingly unwanted Africans.

I admire the accomplishments of Israel and Jews in human history. One of the many attributes of Israel that comes to my mind is the ability to know what goes on in distant lands. Surely, why would Israel choose to send innocent Africans to President Kagame's Rwanda? President Kagame's regime is now globally known for its record of lynching and killing its own citizens at home and abroad, closing space for political activity and independent media, preventing civil society and intellectual activity to thrive, and relentlessly destabilizing the Great Lakes through invasions and proxy wars. Is it possible that Israel, of all nations in the world, would not know these public truths, and hence unknowingly send Africans to Rwanda? If Israel knows the truth but chooses to ignore it out of national interest, what is in the bargain with Rwanda?

When I arrived in Washington DC in 1996 as Rwanda's Ambassador after the 1994 genocide, a first on my order of business was to visit the U.S. Holocaust Memorial Museum. Subsequently I visited Yad Vashem Memorial in Israel. I have, over the years, made friends with many Jews across many organizations. It is easy to identify with Jews because of the Holocaust and the 1994 genocide in Rwanda. These shared experiences have enormously humbled and educated me.

The Jewish Holocaust and the Rwandan genocide need to be understood properly, because President Paul Kagame and the Tutsi minority regime he has built would like to make it a Tutsi-Jewish affair. This obscures the fact that many Hutu have been killed in Rwanda, and the Democratic Republic of Congo, and are not even allowed to remember their own dead, thus making true reconciliation and healing still a distant aspiration among the majority of Rwandans.

Most importantly, making Israel-Rwanda relations, as well as relations between Jews and Rwandans anchored on President Kagame and a clique from the Tutsi minority is both dangerous and unsustainable. It fans the simmering embers of anti-Semitism that one finds lurking behind those who easily find pretext to equate most of Israel's policies and actions, right or wrong, part of a "grand Jewish conspiracy".

As we commemorate the 20th anniversary of the 1994 genocide and massacres, as Rwandans and human beings we are painfully reminded that evil has no religion, nation, sex, race or color. We should feel attracted to the idea of being our brothers and sisters keeper, even when, or especially when, they are as wretched as those Africans being sent to Rwanda. We should feel the same outrage and be persuaded to act to prevent and stop genocide and other human rights abuses, whether the targets are Tutsi, Hutu, or any other humans.

In a letter to his fellow Jews during the Babylonian captivity, the Prophet Jeremiah had this advice:

> "..Also, seek the peace and prosperity of the city to which I have carried you into exile. Pray to the LORD for it, because if it prospers, you too will prosper." (Jeremiah 29:7).

The Africans who have sought refuge among you might in the long run contribute to Israel's peace and prosperity.

Who knows, that Israel is there for Africans for such times as these?

3

THE KAGAME DOCTRINE AFTER 20 YEARS (*March, 2014*)

African leaders have just concluded a mini summit in Luanda, Angola, to discuss the conflict in the Democratic Republic of Congo and the diplomatic showdown between South Africa and Rwanda. It is reported, as usual, that a "Luanda Declaration" was signed, and President Zuma and President Kagame "agreed" to talk to "resolve" the impasse between their two countries.

The latest quarrel between South Africa and Rwanda is due to the assassination of Colonel Patrick Karegeya in South Africa on 12/31/2013 and another attempted assassination on General Kayumba Nyamwasa a couple of weeks ago.

Is this new ground for hope, or it is the usual diplomatic hype, postponing the problem to a later date? This writer firmly believes it is the latter.

A good foreign policy champions, defends and protects a country's (read people's) national interests. It seeks friends and builds alliances. It aims to contain enemies, and prevent war. When war becomes inevitable, a country should be able to win it by having good and reliable friends on its side.

A poor and landlocked country like Rwanda should not easily pick quarrels with neighbors who share history, culture, and through whose territory its exports and imports flow. When such a poor country is dependent on aid, a country's leadership should have professional humility to accept "begging with a purpose," to overcome the people's poverty and begging in the long term.

As Paul Kagame's reign of terror celebrates its 20th anniversary, its quest to make enemies continues unabated. Its domestic policy displays exceptional brutality against Rwandan citizens.

Since coming to power in 1994, Kagame's RPF regime has killed as a matter of policy within and outside Rwanda. The regime's criminal record is long enough to cause outrage and response: the shooting down of President Habyarimana's plane which triggered genocide; the murder of Rwandan bishops and priests (1994); the Robert Gersony Report (1994); the Kibeho massacres (1995); the UN Mapping Report of 2010 that documented war crimes, crimes against humanity, and even possible acts of genocide against Hutu; and, assassinations of opponents in Rwanda and abroad, just to mention a few.

Paul Kagame's foreign policy is predominantly and consistently belligerent. In 1994, it assassinated the President of Burundi, Cyprien Ntaryamira. In 2001, it assassinated the President of the Democratic Republic of Congo, Laurent Kabila, having invaded that country twice and still maintaining its presence through proxies like M23. Close to 6 million Congolese people have perished due to Kagame's policies and actions in DRC.

Paul Kagame's troops fought Ugandan troops in the DRC in 2000. He has picked fights with Tanzania and now South Africa. He has fought Zimbabwe, Angola and Namibia. He has castigated international human rights organizations, and western governments when they have criticized his domestic and foreign policies.

How should we characterize Paul Kagame's foreign policy?

First, it is anti-Hutu, anti-Tutsi and anti-Twa. In short, it is an anti-people, anti-democratic, sectarian domestic policy. Its human rights record is outrageous. It kills, jails, intimidates, makes people disappear, or exiles them.

Second, it is a militaristic regime that has a facade of a civilian government whose formal institutions have been usurped by a narrow clique of a "minority within a minority," i.e Tutsi military officers within a minority ethnic group.

Third, it is founded on grand deception and intimidation. The regime has falsified Rwanda's history to suit its agenda, and consistently hides its role in contributing to the tragedies of modern day Rwanda and the Great Lakes region (genocide, war crimes and crimes against humanity in Rwanda and DRC).

Fourth, it preys on the guilt of the international community, for its failures before, during and after the 1994 genocide. Because of this guilt, the international community has either been silenced or wooed into an unholy alliance with Kagame.

Fifth, it is belligerent and aggressive within the Great Lakes region. Since 1994, the regime has fought or made enemies with the Democratic Republic of Congo, Zimbabwe, Namibia, Angola, South Africa, Uganda and now, sadly but predictably, Tanzania.

Sixth, it is an anti-African foreign policy. The Kagame doctrine is founded on cheap and opportunistic arrogance that has no respect for the genuine interests of the African people. He now abuses the West because his longtime allies now find him an inconvenient and embarrassing burden. He has adapted a pan-Africanist language, while he has worked, openly and secretly, against Africa's interests.

Seventh, it is an immoral foreign policy, founded on the premise that opponents, whether heads of state or ordinary citizens, must die or be jailed.

The Kagame doctrine is not simply wrong. It is anti-Rwandan, militaristic, deceptive, predatory, belligerent, anti-African and immoral. In short, it is dangerous for Rwanda, the Great Lakes region, Africa and the international community.

The Kagame Doctrine is a malignant cancer that spreads day by day. Appeasement and palliative treatment may give us a deceptive and temporary relief. What is needed is aggressive surgery to contain, stop and remove President Paul Kagame and his clique from power.

In the medium to long term, Rwandan will prosper and be at peace at home and with neighbors only when 1) freedom and democracy reign, 2) security institutions are rescued from the hands of a Tutsi clique, and 3) justice for all Rwandans prevails at last. This will inevitably be painful, but ultimately save Rwanda and her neighbors from the impending civil war, and in the worst-case scenario, another genocide.

4

RWANDA'S CRIMINAL NETWORK: FREQUENTLY ASKED
QUESTIONS (*January, 2014*)

*W*ho are the leaders and members of the criminal network?

(Note that except for the Prime Minister, members of this network
and the support system are all Tutsi. The First Lady, Mrs. Jeannette
Kagame, informally occupies the second place in command and
control of this criminal network)

1. President Paul Kagame

2. Mrs. Jeanette Kagame

3. Major General Jack Nziza, "Inspector General" of Rwanda
Defence Forces

4. Lt. General James Kabarebe, Minister of Defence

5. Lt.General Karenzi Karake, Head of National Security Service

6. Lt. General Ibingira, Commander of Reserve Forces

7. Col. Emmanuel Ndahiro, Former Head, National Security
Service and Kagame's personal doctor

8. Major General Richard Rutatina, Commander Special Forces

9. Emmanuel Gasana, Commissioner General of Police

10. Col. Francis Mutiganda, Head of External Intelligence

11. Faustin Kalisa, Commissioner of Police

12. Lt.Col.Franco Rutagengwa, Director of Military Intelligence

13. Lt. Col. Francis Gakwerere (Chief Assassin at-large)

14. Col Dan Munyuza, Deputy Commissioner General of Police

Where does the money to sustain the criminal network come from?

1. John Rwangombwa, Minister of Finance

2. Claver Gatete, Governor of Central Bank

3. Ben Kagarama, Commissioner of Rwanda Revenue Authority

4. Jack Nkusi Kayonga, CEO of Rwanda Development Bank and Executive Chairman of Crystal Ventures

5. Eugene Haguma, CEO of the Horizon Group

6. Dr. Agnes Binagwaho, Minister of Health (largest recipient of foreign aid)

Who are the foreigners who defend and protect the criminal network abroad, and mobilize the resources from donors and private sector?

1. Bill Clinton, Former US President

2. Tony Blair, Former British Prime Minister

3. Rick Warren, Pastor of Saddleback Church, California, USA

4. Rabbi Shmuley Boteach, an American Orthodox rabbi

5. Michael Fairbanks, consultant for President Kagame and Co-Founder of SEVEN Fund

6. Andrew Mwenda, owner of the Ugandan newspaper *The Independent* sponsored by the Kigali regime

Who are the amplifiers who legitimize state crimes?

1. Pierre Habumuremyi, Prime Minister

2. Louise Mushikiwabo, Minister of Foreign Affairs

3. The New Times, State owned and operated newspaper

4. The Christian Church (Protestant denominations, especially the Anglican Church)

What is the role of Rwanda's embassies abroad in criminal activities?

They are the staging ground for organization, execution and cover up of the criminal activities, especially of assassination of political dissidents and intimidating of Rwandan exiles in general.

Who are the bilateral allies of Kagame's regime?

1. The United States Government
2. The United Kingdom Government
3. President Yoweri Museveni, Uganda.

5

LET US CELEBRATE NELSON MANDELA (*December, 2013*)

Mandela believed

Mandela saw further, deeper, and wider

Mandela planted the seeds of hope in times of suffering

Mandela sacrificed for his people because he cherished their value

Mandela's love (Ubuntu) transcended human barriers

Mandela's large heart embraced his former enemies

Mandela unified and reconciled a broken nation

Mandela was an imperfect and mortal being like you and me...

AND...

Mandela was a great African

Mandela was an exemplary and humble leader

Mandela was a caring human being

Because he lived

He made Africans proud

We all can face tomorrow with hope

Because Mandela lives forever...

MAY HIS SOUL REST IN ETERNAL PEACE!

6

THE TRAGEDY OF GOMA (*November, 2012*)

For the last several months Rwandans, Congolese, Africans and the international community have watched as the predictable drama from Kagame's regime plays out once again in the Kivu region of Eastern Democratic Republic of Congo. With the birth of M23, the Kigali regime re-engineered the mutation of an old proxy force (CNDP) into a new one with the same agenda: 1) weaken DRC 2) loot its natural resources 3) pretend that Rwanda can now solve the problem by paying lip-service to negotiations 4) deceive the world that Rwanda is after Rwandan armed groups , especially FDLR and 5) use this presence in DRC to manipulate the international community against looking at the problems within Rwanda itself. In all this President Kagame's trademarks remain deception, total disregard for human life, and disrespect to the international community.

First, where is Africa in all this? It is African countries, notably through African Union, that chose Rwanda to represent the continent at the UN Security Council. Like Rwanda, DRC has been bleeding for several years, and has lost 6 million of its citizens due to Kagame's wars of plunder and killings. Can't Africa save DRC and Rwanda from the most vicious and brutal dictator since Idi

Amin?

Second, the United Nations has a peacekeeping operation in DRC: over 20,000 personnel and an annual budget of close to 1.5 billion US dollars. What is the United Nations doing in DRC if it cannot defend a small African city like GOMA, and protect its women and children? The United Nations Secretary General Ban Ki-Moon has become too close to President Kagame that he has lost objectivity in dealing with the crisis in DRC. In 2010, when the Mapping Report was published, Ban Ki -Moon hurriedly packed his bags and went to Kigali to beg Kagame not to pull out Rwandan troops from Sudan. The Mapping Report has been shelved. Now as the Goma drama unfolded, Ban Ki-Moon called Kagame, pleading that the latter (Kagame) "use his influence" to stop the advance of M23 on Goma." Incredible! The same United Nations has rewarded Kagame with a seat on the Security Council, and is now failing to hold him and his officers accountable for the violations of international law.

What is the stand of the United States and British Governments on the unfolding tragedy in Goma? Rwanda has invaded a neighboring country and violated DRC's sovereignty and territorial integrity. President Kagame's regime is brutal and dictatorial at home, and belligerent in the Great Lakes region. Washington and London have been Kagame's allies since 1994, and friendship with powerful nations has made him more intransigent and willing to undertake costly risks. It is important for Washington and London to re-evaluate their relationship with Kagame to avoid the "French-Rwanda" disease. In the early 1990's, France was able and yet unwilling to read the signals showing the last days of a regime, committed sins of omission and commission, and has regretted since. France was capable of playing a good influence through a friendly regime of President Habyarimana. It chose not to. The consequences were catastrophic.

Washington and London have a narrow window of opportunity to stop and reverse their unquestioning policies towards Rwanda's Paul Kagame. Failure to do so in the short and medium term will contribute to even worse tragedies in Rwanda and the Great lakes region. The tide of change may not seem evident to the uncaring, distracted or biased eyes. President Kagame is now the butcher of Rwanda and DRC. He will certainly go. The question is, will he do so peacefully or with unprecedented bloodshed in Rwanda and the region? If Washington and London cannot help Rwandans and Congolese to end this bloodshed and human suffering, at least they should not make matters worse by keeping silent or supporting Kagame as he puts the whole region on fire. It is time for Washington and London to make a choice.

The Rwandan and Congolese people must, as a matter of urgency and survival, work together to save themselves and their motherlands. Rwandans and Congolese people must seek the solidarity of Africans in the struggle against a minority clique under Kagame's rule. Rwandans and Congolese must seek partners in the international community who regard respect for human rights, peace, freedom and shared human progress as cornerstones of international relations.

It is highly probable that by the time I wake up Goma will be in the hands of Rwanda's troops masquerading as M23. After all, Rwanda has deployed its special forces, and almost a division of its armed forces, its equipment and other resources to take Goma. Rwanda may be then enticed to take Bukavu in South Kivu, or even be lured into DRC's tempting belly. Even then, Kagame must know this: it will be a futile exercise since, like all his ventures in DRC, he will be forced to abandon it, leaving with bags of Coltan, diamonds and gold, and behind him a trail of blood, tears and sweat of Rwandans and Congolese. DRC will, sooner than later, prove to be Paul Kagame's Achilles heel.

7

EXIT STRATEGIES OUT OF GOMA: A FIVE-POINT
AGENDA (*November, 2012*)

The international community (read: western powers) have put
pressure on Kagame to have his creation and proxy, M23,
withdraw from Goma. President Kabila is being pressured to talk
to M23, to listen to their grievances. As we have argued, the
problems of eastern DRC are partly a Congolese problem of
internal weaknesses and, in this latest war, largely due to Rwanda's
internal political and human rights crisis. If the international
community is asking Kabila to talk to a Rwanda-created and
Rwanda-backed organization (mainly of Tutsi), wouldn't it be
logical that Kagame would be pressured to listen to the legitimate
grievances of Rwandans (Hutu and Tutsi) in both the peaceful and
armed opposition? Kagame has totally closed the political space in
Rwanda, imprisoned, killed or forced into exile opposition political
leaders, journalists and human rights activists.

In Rwanda, an exclusively Tutsi clique of military officers run the
show on behalf of President Kagame and his family. These are the
same officers (James Kabarebe, Charles Kayonga, and the
notorious Jack Nziza) that the UN Group of experts report has

cited as being at the heart of the M23 rebellion. They are the same officers whom Kagame used to shoot down the plane in which the

President of Rwanda and Burundi were killed on April 6, 1994. They are the same officers that Kagame used to assassinate President Laurent Kabila of DRC in 2001. They are the same officers that are at the heart of the horrendous crimes committed against Hutu in Rwanda and DRC, which were described in the UN Mapping Report of 2010 and other previous reports.

We have entered a period of high risk and escalation in Rwanda and the Great Lakes region. Within Rwanda, we are probably 2 to 3 years to a major event, which could escalate into a full civil war. The political space has become completely closed, with moderate voices dead, in jail or in exile. The regime has become ever more illegitimate, intransigent, and aggressive. Power is vested in the hands of President Kagame and his wife, and a few Tutsi military officers who run both the formal and informal government. President Kagame and his top three military officers (James Kabarebe, Charles Kayonga and Jack Nziza) have ceaselessly turned to DRC, the latest venture being the M23, itself with high potential to escalate into a full civil war that could easily turn regional and ugly. Many people in Rwanda, DRC, Great Lakes region, Africa and the International Community are asking about the endgame in the current crisis in DRC.

Although the current problem in the eastern DRC has a Congolese component, the M23 saga is Rwanda's (and secondarily, Uganda's) creation. You cannot solve, once and for all, the M23 problem without dealing with Rwanda's own political crisis, and re-evaluating the west's unquestioning support to President Kagame and President Museveni. Short of new and innovative ways in the thinking process, policy, and action to underpin diplomatic, political and aid-related initiatives, withdrawal from Goma will be a temporary and futile measure, as we shall then wait for the resurgence of another round of violent conflict.

The international community, notably the US and the UK, may consider the following five measures to facilitate a sustainable movement out of the current DRC crisis:

1. Immediately initiate a contact group to spearhead a two-track peace process (DRC and Rwanda). The contact group should include the United States, the United Kingdom, France, Belgium, South Africa, Uganda and Tanzania. The UK and US are key because, until now, that is what President Kagame cares for. The two western powers have also protected Kagame from calls for accountability with regard to his endless and costly DRC ventures, human rights, and lack of political freedoms in Rwanda etc. Belgium and France were engaged with previous regimes in Rwanda, and may have a few lessons they have learnt with regard

to Rwanda. Tanzania has the institutional memory since it
facilitated the Arusha peace process. South Africa is an important
regional player. Uganda should be included simply because it
could be a spoiler if left out.

2. The contact group should be brutally candid towards Kabila,
Museveni and especially Kagame. Yesterday, as I listened to
African Union Chairman Zuma and US Secretary of State Clinton,
I was saddened and disheartened by the fact that neither could
summon the courage to call a spade a spade, name Rwanda as a
culprit and put Kagame to shame. As a young doctor, I was taught
that the pathway to healing necessitates telling the patient what the
diagnosis is, and empowering him/her to take the lead in a healing
process. Mrs. Zuma and Mr. Clinton highlight an ailment that
afflicts the international system: when convenient, be silent or
conceal the truth. Kagame loves that! The contact group
collectively has substantive leverage to bring to the table. The
members of the contact group understand the current power
dynamics in Rwanda. They appreciate the consequences of
maintaining the status quo and inaction in Rwanda, DRC, the Great
Lakes region, and to international peace and security. Yes, the
United States and UK may be focused on their security interests in
Somalia and Sudan, and prone to blackmail from Kagame and
Museveni. However, failure to act fairly in the Great Lakes region
risks creating more enemies in Africa. This would be counter-

productive and dangerous.

3. The contact group should directly engage Rwandans, Congolese and Ugandans struggling for freedom and justice. A timid international community that will not care for African people, and will only look at a country's interests through the eyes of Kagame, Kabila and Museveni is a recipe for cyclical conflict and disaster. The thousands of civil and political groups that are calling for change in these countries are imperfect, but still they are indispensable stakeholders. In the case of Rwanda, President Kagame must unconditionally talk to the opposition whether armed or not. You make peace with enemies and opponents. The international community must support efforts that promote genuine dialogue, unity, reconciliation and healing within Rwanda and DRC, and in the various Diasporas. It is no good value for money when billions are spent in development projects when many in Rwanda and DRC feel they are marginalized.

4. Africans and the rest of the international community must make sure that those who have committed horrendous human rights abuses, war crimes, crimes against humanity and genocide are held accountable. Specifically, the United States and United Kingdom governments should stop protecting President Kagame and his officers who have committed serious crimes in Rwanda and the DRC. Those in the World Bank, IMF, DFID , USAID, and the aid industry who tell Rwandans that Kagame is fine because he is

efficient in using aid are playing a bad influence since
development without rights is both sham and unsustainable.

5. The African Union and the United Nations, since they have
condemned themselves to be ineffectual observers in the DRC and
Rwanda tragedies, should at least jointly and urgently convene a
conference to consider a "Marshal Plan" for the Great Lakes
Region to motivate the tens of millions of unemployed youth and
women who are both victims and tools of state and non-state
actors. The United Nations and the African Union should avail
resources for participants from civil society and the political
opposition to attend. Since the international community is asking
President Kabila to listen to the grievance of M23, when will the
African Union and the United Nations listen to the grievance of the
African people?

Sooner than later the costly, redundant and scandal-prone UN
peacekeepers in DRC will be asked to abandon what has become
an embarrassing operation. The Congolese people will, as usual,
and like the Rwandans and Somalis now and in the past, continue
to struggle to survive. The challenge to resist Rwanda's (and
Uganda's) attempts to promote secession and plunder of DRC is
primarily a Congolese one. All Rwandans, DRC's neighbors,
Africans and the international community should, however, have
an interest in preventive measures before it is too late. A window

of opportunity does exist, but it is closing fast. We must act innovatively, and together, now.

8

A DANGEROUS REPEAT OFFENDER ON THE WAY TO HIS FALL*(September, 2012)*

President Kagame leads a busy and eventful life of a repeat offender. Yesterday he had his security forces kidnap Alex Bakunzibake, Vice President of PS Imberakuri. If Alex is lucky and survives death at the hands of Kagame's hangmen, he will languish in jail, alongside Victoire Ingabire, President of FDU-Inkingi, Bernard Ntaganda,Chairman and Founder of PS Imberakuri, Deo Mushayidi of PDP, and many other innocent Rwandans incarcerated for their beliefs and struggle for freedom. It is also possible that Alex will be released, when his tormentors suddenly realise that a crime committed in broad daylight may turn out to be an expensive mistake. The assasssination of Sendashonga and Lizinde, the gruesome beheading of Rwisereka, the assassination of Ingabire and Rugambagye, the assassination attempt on General Nyamwasa, and the multiple stabbings on the young Frank Ntwari in South Africa only point to a sick and primitive serial killer on rampage.

In his cupboard, Kagame has many skeletons: President Habyarimana of Rwanda, President Ntaryamira of Burundi, President Kabila of DRC, millions of Rwandans and Congolese killed in Rwanda and DRC, Rwandans assassinated abroad since 1994, and his thirst for killing at home and abroad continues. International reports and investigations on his crimes do not deter him. He has either ignored them, or manipulated them with the help of accomplices in the international community. Such has been the fate of the Gersony Report, the Mapping Report, the French investigation, and the ICTR. He has repeatedly abused the sovereignty and territorial integrity of DRC, causing millions of deaths, without being brought to account. Only recently has the world shyly come to realise that Kagame is not only dangerous to Rwandans, but to Rwanda's neighbors as well. When Rwandans took him to the International Criminal Court at The Hague two weeks ago, he said, "who cares?". Taken to court in Oklahoma and Iowa states in the United States over the shooting down of the Habyarimana plane, he can only claim presidential immunity as his only defence.

Yet, for all the show of public bravado, Kagame is increasingly an isolated, frustrated, angry, insecure and dangerous man who is determined to drag a whole nation and its 11 million citizens to another avoidable tragedy. The United Nations accused him of starting and fueling the M23 rebellion in DRC. The United States, United Kingdom, Holland, AfDB, Sweden, and Germany suspended aid. SADC gave its warning to Kigali. In response, the

Kigali regime ironically amplified its harsh anti-west rhetoric, attempting to mobilize Africans whom Kagame has long despised and undermined while he was the west's favored cry-baby. The regime has even set up the so-called Agaciro Development Fund, thereby coercing contributions from already impoverished Rwandans. Kagame's wealth and scandalously luxurious life meanwhile remain untouched.

Kagame has said the west has put him in a corner, against the wall, and can only fight back. Rather than stop Rwanda's losses, he is beating drums of war and violence. The truth is, he has put himself in a point of no return. He has pushed Rwandans and Congolese against the wall. Slowly but surely the veil of fear is crumbling, and Rwandans and Congolese have nothing to lose but their misery. Killing and jailing more Rwandans will not save him. On the contrary, more repression fuels anger. When mobilization and organization attain a critical mass, anger and fear will turn into portent weapons of peaceful change. When (not if) this time comes, and each day brings us closer to the endgame, Kagame will be at the mercy of the people and the rule of law.

RNC salutes you, freedom fighters of PS-Imberakuri and FDU-Inkingi.

We shall win!

9

PAUL KAGAME'S ENDLESS DIPLOMATIC GAMBLES
(*February, 2012*)

The saga between Kagame and France continues. It is a familiar story that sometimes sounds like a children's fairy tale. The latest is France recalling its Ambassador to Kigali, whom many have referred to as a French RPF cadre. Reason? Kagame does not want the new French nominee to the diplomatic post in Kigali because "she is too close to the French Foreign Minister", Alain Juppe, whom Kagame considers "hostile to Rwanda's interests!" Judging from the past rhythm of the Kagame-Sarkozy dance, Kagame throws a tantrum and then Paris finally backs down and does Kagame's bidding. Kagame expelled the French Ambassador a couple of years ago, and the next time Sarkozy was in Kigali. Kagame daily insults the French and then they invite him to France. He denounces the French as the accomplices to the 1994 genocide in Rwanda (Read Mutsinzi and Mucyo reports) and the Trevidic report comes out at best lukewarm and at worst plays into the Kagame hands with respect to the shooting down of the Habyarimana plane.

Kagame's whole diplomatic venture with France is a gamble to prevent the truth coming out with regard to the terrorist crime he committed by ordering the shooting down of the Habyarimana plane. He knows that his legitimacy and future hang on this decisive landmark event. He will spend any political and economic resources to manipulate or blackmail the French and the international public opinion to frustrate and subvert the course of justice. When any pretense of civility fails, he will resort to primitive violence.

Kagame has absolute power in Rwanda, and he often boasts that he can always do whatever he wants. He calls his personal interests "Rwanda's interests". He thinks and acts as if Rwanda's national interests are synonymous with his personal interests. He is Rwanda. Rwanda is him. He has forgotten or ignored that France is another sovereign country? If other countries accept Kagame's diplomats, some of whom are really his houseboys and girls, or sometimes agents on criminal errands to kill refugees, who is he to question France's legitimate choice of their diplomats?

The one-million dollar question is why France (or Sarkozy?) would pursue a counter-productive or futile policy of appeasement on Kagame? Kagame will never change his posture on France unless Paris proclaims him innocent of the crime of shooting down of the plane. Moreover, even when they do that, he will ask them to kneel before him and ask for forgiveness for having been accomplices in the 1994 genocide. Like the English saying, they are damned if they do, and damned if they don't. If France is operating out of the guilt of the past like the rest of the international community, they better outgrow it and deal with Kagame firmly, in the interest of Rwanda and all of its citizens. If they have other legitimate interests in Rwanda and the Great Lakes region, they are placing their eggs in one broken basket. Kagame is on the way out. He has outlived his usefulness, and has become a break to progress in Rwanda and the Great Lakes region. France needs to exorcise its demons on Rwanda, and be bold enough to deal with the emerging Rwandan pro-democracy voices. That is where the future lies.

Accepting Kagame's belligerent diplomatic gambles is a non-sustainable basis for bilateral Franco-Rwanda relations; it is also an extremely dangerous policy. It has far-reaching and negative consequences for Rwanda, the Great Lakes region, Africa and international peace and security.

As the game of brinkmanship unfolds let us wait and see who blinks first: Sarkozy or Kagame?

10

A GENERAL WITHOUT GENERALS (*February, 2012*)

General Paul Kagame's recent "arrests" of his notorious generals and colonels (Ibingira, Rutatina, Munyuza, et al) left Rwandans and the international community speculating as to what the errant General Kagame is up. You might recall that last year we tried to make sense of his unintelligent reshuffle in which Karenzi, Rutatina and Munyuza, officers that he distrusts, hates and despises, were to head key security organisations and departments (National Security Agency, Directorate of Military Intellegence, and External Intelligence). We have been proven right. General Kagame's moves, attitude, behavior and actions are more acts of desperation than coherent strategy. He may boast that he will rise and never fall, but he is a general without real generals.

Ten Things that Can Happen to General Paul Kagame's Generals:

1. Inconsequential Promotions and Deployments:

The greatest danger signal to a general in Rwanda is when he is asked to become a Minister of Defence or head the National Security Service (NSS). Lt. Generals Kayumba Nyamwasa and Marcel Gatsinzi have been there. Currently James Kabarebe occupies the glamorous post of Minister of Defence, essentially retired out of active military service. General Kagame is his own Defence Minister and Chief Intelligence Officer. He would never sub-contract this function to anybody.

2. Deport to a Diplomatic Mission:

Lt. General Kayumba Nyamwasa was banished to India as Ambassador at a time when Kagame was looking for every avenue to marginalise or kill him.

3. "Agatebe" (reduced to being redundant):

Generals will be humiliated with trumped up charges (General Muhire, corruption; General Karenzi, sexual immorality, Rwigamba, corruption etc). Without support from the state, the officers are impoverished and left to beg for mercy from General Kagame.

4. Criminalised:

General Kagame has criminalized his Generals. From the killing of President Habyarimana, President Ntaryamira, President Laurent Kabila, the crimes of Kibeho and Democratic Republic of Congo, the assassinations of his comrades in the RPA, Seth Sendashonga, Lizinde, Kayumba assassination attempt, and many others, General Kagame has corrupted otherwise good officers to become criminals. Now they are trapped with him as co-criminals.

5. Send to DRC on commercial errands:

With an appetite for DRC's mineral wealth, General Kagame has sent his Generals to loot for him. When their actions become public knowledge, he disowns and "arrests" them. Traitor-in-Chief becomes law and discipline enforcer, prosecutor and Judge.

6. Blackmail:

General Kagame uses Generals to spy on each other, as they compete for his ear, attention and favors. He keeps dossiers on them and at the opportune moment blackmails them into silence and forced loyalty to him.

7. Apologize:

Like in the Stalinist era, Generals who have fallen from grace are asked by Kagame's coterie of civilian and military (RPF and RDF) officers to apologize for sins they did not commit and abandon "bad influences." Inyumba, Tito Rutaremara, James Kabarebe, Kayonga, et al have tried this on Nyamwasa, Karegeya, and many others.

8. Start a war:

General Kagame has always been the General who leads from the safety of the rear. He does not care who goes to war, and whether they survive or not. He has made his Generals behave like automatons who must fight his futile wars in Congo, wars without purpose, wars of plunder, and very costly wars in human terms. While Kagame's generals are 99.99% Tutsi, the expendable men are mostly Hutu.

9. Demobilize:

General Kagame takes Rwanda Defence Forces as his personal army. Frequently, after beating officers, he chases them out of "his army."

10. Kill them:

Ultimately, if a General cannot bend to Kagame's way, he must be killed. The cases of Nyamwasa and Karegeya illustrate this point. Kagame uses meetings with officers to hammer this point to his Generals and other officers.

Napoleon once said that an army moves on its stomach. He probably over-emphasized the stomach part and forgot that an army, and its generals as its leaders, must have a national purpose and a conscience that defends a people, not the commercial and personal interests of a dictator. General Kagame has destroyed Rwanda's Generals. He has become a General without Generals. The generals have become an endangered species. Only they and the Rwandan citizens will save them from extinction.

11

A STATE WITHOUT A STATESMAN (*December, 2011*)

It was an annual event that has been erroneously baptised national dialogue. It is neither national nor even a dialogue. Paul Kagame and his RPF-a minority in a political and ethnic sense- use the occasion to harass Rwandans who are not in their ever-diminishing clique, and foreigners who raise questions about Rwanda's current crisis of human rights and governance. Kagame's monologue was almost solely directed against all foreigners- mainly the United States (whose Ambassador, Susan Rice, criticised Rwanda's lack of democracy, press freedoms and abuse of human rights) and Belgium. His list of enemies also included the usual suspects: journalists and human rights activists. It is, however, to Ambassador Rice's criticism that Kagame hurled harsh words and insults: intruder, nonsense, joker, liar, double standards, masquaraders, etc.

Kagame's speech is very hard to analyse. In the past, I have worked very hard to help President Kagame with his speeches, both on the content aspects, as well as on the delivery side. He proved to be a very poor student, even at the hands of people with more expertise than mine. I was visiting friends this weekend when somebody tried to convince me to listen to his latest speech. I was hesitant, for I have generally stopped reading or listening to Kagame's speeches. He lies a lot. He has no respect for Rwandans. For the many problems that Rwanda has, he either is the source, complicates them, or has no solutions to offer. I succumbed to my friend's pressure and went through the agony of listening to thirty minutes of a very painful reminder that Rwanda has become a state without a statesman.

First, his poverty of ideas comes out, loud and clear. Listening to him, at some point I thought I was listening to a re-incarnated Idi Amin. He wonders whether Rwandans are deaf, they have nothing to say, or somebody prevents from speaking. Then he jumps to the late King Mutara Rudahigwa. Then to Africa and the begging business. On an and on..In psychiatry, they call it a "fleeting of ideas", typical of states in which a patient has both grand delusions of themselves, and paranoia that everyone is out against them, and ideas that seem not to have connections.

Second, his lies, deceptions and denials are all too evident. He attempts to rally people around himself by using, genocide, Bagosora, and the failures of the international community. He pretends that he does not know how the same international community he now insults (especially the USA and UK) has protected him from accountability for war crimes, crimes against humanity (UN Mapping Report), terrorism (shooting down the

Habyarimana plane,). Otherwise, by now Kagame would be languishing in jail, alongside Bagosora. His remarks are calculated to once again intimidate the international community, now that there is a fresh and irresistible momentum to have him account for his crimes.

Third, his sense of frustration and anger comes through in form of harsh words and insults. We know this type of behaviour from ourselves or our children when caught red-handed. However, Kagame's is a special case. Rwandans and foreigners need to understand that Kagame's mindset is that of serial killer and mass murderer, and stop dealing with him as a normal rational being. He is self-absorbed in a world of his own, and the entire Rwandan system re-enforces a distorted image of himself. The emperor is naked, but the clapping multitudes keep on telling him he is wonderfully made and dressed. Kagame is a like a reckless driver on a high way, driving in the opposite direction to the traffic. He is over speeding, his passengers (the hostages) hold their breath but still smile and clap. Other drivers are wondering what is going on, as the police scramble to stop the mad driver. Over loudspeakers mounted on the Rwanda bus, he asks, "we ni nani?" "who are you?"

In history and in modern times, effective statesmen do three things. When they are born and forged in difficult times, they help their fellow citizens to overcome fear. They accomplish this, by combining a sufficient dose of tension so that people act out their comfort zones, but making sure, they are not paralysed by fear. Second, a statesman embodies the hope of a people, of a whole nation. Without such a hope, without such a vision, people perish (in Kinyarwanda, bapfa bahagaze). Last, and most importantly, the statesman is large-hearted, to accommodate all his/her people/ nation with their faults and strengths.

President Kagame is no such statesman. He has subjected the whole nation of Rwanda, Rwanda's neighbors, and the international community to fear. He is a mean-spirited man who takes pride in killing and dividing Rwandans. Concluding his monologue, Kagame said he has never been vague in his life, "what you see is what you get." In short, he is telling us, "you can die, be fearful, hopeless, languish in jails and exile....I do not give a damn..who are you??".

Bismarck, the German Chancellor of "blood and iron" who unified Germany is quoted to have stated that statesmanship consisted of listening carefully to the footsteps of God through history and walking with him a few steps of the way. Kagame has neither the humility nor the capability to listen to God's footsteps, nor to walk with Him even one step in the right direction.

Now that Kagame is against Rwandans, foreigners and God, who is for him? His speech will be counted among his worst and last, and surely a signal that for him and us, the final countdown to the end has begun.

12

A HOUSE WITH MANY ROOMS

God has given us an amazingly beautiful country, and inherently good people who are prone to do destructive things. We are trying to rebuild our Father's house that is currently hurting.

First, we have to agree on the PLAN of the house. Everyone is invited to make a contribution on the vision of a Rwanda we have for the future.

Second, we have to BUILD the house together, from each according to his/her ability.

Third, we have to LIVE in the house, all of us, the good and the bad.

Fourth, we have to agree on the RULES to guide all of us to live in this house without being a danger to each other and to our neighbours. Everyone must be equal before the rules, even the rulers!

Last, but not least, together we have to PROTECT our house, just in case we are tempted to destroy it again, as we have done in the past till now. Rwandan territory is small. However, Rwanda is more than physical territory. If Rwandans can have big hearts and big ideas, there is enough room for all of us (Hutu, Tutsi, Twa), now and forever. The job of rebuilding Rwanda will never be perfect, nor will it ever be completely finished. Each generation must do its part. Let us begin now.

13

RWANDA'S RED SEA MOMENT (*October, 2011*)

So, here we are, like the Israelites in ancient times, trapped

between our own Pharaoh (Kagame) pursuing us and our own red

sea (challenges) before us. Among us are people who are fearful,

even preferring to go back to captivity. Among us are those that

are easily distracted and deceived by little idols we have created

for ourselves (material stuff) forgetting the abundant promise that

awaits us beyond the red sea. There are those who have hard hearts

and would not wish to believe in the good news that we are diverse

families, yet destined for a great promise for one strong and

indivisible nation. Then we also have time to grumble about this

and that. Fear, idolatry, hard and unbelieving hearts, and

grumblings are what is delaying our own deliverance from this

desert we have been in for too long. We must conquer these

enemies first, and God will frustrate and defeat Kagame's schemes

before our own eyes.

Seven things to think about:

1. Believe and receive the promise that Rwandans will reach the
promised land
2. Let us determine as quickly as possible how many were. In

Rwanda, we are told we are 11 million. Outside Rwanda how many are refugees, non-refugees, country by country and we?

3. We shall be mobilised and organized community by community, and have community leaders chosen by their own communities.

4. Be light on "stuff." A good soldier travels light. Our spending priorities are our children's education, shelter and basic upkeep. The rest should be invested into our common future, for our children and grandchildren. The place to begin is the journey we have begun. Freeze unnecessary consumption.

5. Talk to your children in simple terms why this journey is for them, and how important it is. If you do not talk to them now, and yourself, who will and when? The pharaoh spends fortunes polluting and deceiving the minds of our children. It is time to give our children a different education.

6. Women: gather your treasures of gold and silver. These will be handy on rainy days we anticipate ahead.

7. Reach out to the friends we have made during our captivity, the ones who welcomed us, fed us, and clothed us when we were pitiful and dejected strangers in foreign lands. They are with us on this journey. When we reach home, our land shall be their land too.

Above all, let us struggle with song and joy. Aren't we glad that we are the chosen generation to take our people out of captivity? Can there be a task more important and more satisfying?

14

A CONFESSION

PAUL KAGAME KILLED PRESIDENT JUVENAL HABYARIMANA, PRESIDENT CYPRIEN NTARYAMIRA OF BURUNDI, DEOGRATIAS NSABIMANA, ELIE SAGATWA, THADDEE BAGARAGAZA, JUVENAL RENZAHO, EMMANUEL AKINGENEYE, BERNARD CIZA, CYRIAQUE SIMBIZI, JACKY HERAUD, JEAN PIERRE MINABERRY AND JEAN-MICHEL PERRINE

On August 4, 1993, in Arusha, Tanzania, the Government of Rwanda and the Rwandese Patriotic Front signed the Arusha Peace Agreement. The provisions of the agreement included a commitment to principles of the rule of law, democracy, national unity, pluralism, the respect of fundamental freedoms and the rights of the individual. The agreement further had provisions on power-sharing, formation of a one and single National Army and a new National Gendarmerie from forces of the two warring parties; and a definitive solution to the problem of Rwandan refugees.

On April 6, 1994, at 8:25 p.m., the Falcon 50 jet of the President of the Republic of Rwanda, registration number "9XR-NN", on its return from a summit meeting in DAR-ES-SALAAM, Tanzania, as it was on approach to Kanombe International Airport in KIGALI, Rwanda, was shot down. All on board, including President Juvenal Habyarimana, President Cyprien Ntaryamira of Burundi, their entire entourage and flight crew died.

The death of President Juvenal Habyarimana triggered the start of genocide that targeted Tutsi and Hutu moderates, and the resumption of civil war between RPF and the Government of Rwanda. The RPF's sad and false narrative from that time on has been that Hutu extremists within President Habyarimana's camp shot down the plane to derail the implementation of the Arusha Peace Agreement and to find a pretext to start the genocide in which over 800,000 Rwandans died in just 100 days. This narrative has become a predominant one in some international circles, among scholars, and in some human rights organizations.

The truth must now be told. Paul Kagame, then overall commander of the Rwandese Patriotic Army, the armed wing of the Rwandese Patriotic Front, was personally responsible for the shooting down of the plane. In July 1994, Paul Kagame himself, with characteristic callousness and much glee, told me that he was responsible for shooting down the plane.

Despite public denials, the fact of Kagame's culpability in this crime is also a public "secret" within RPF and RDF circles. Like many others in the RPF leadership, I enthusiastically sold this deceptive story line, especially to foreigners who by and large came to believe it, even when I knew that Kagame was the culprit in this crime.

The political and social atmosphere during the period from the signing of the Arusha Accords in August 1993 was highly explosive, and the nation was on edge. By killing President Habyarimana, Paul Kagame introduced a wild card in an already fragile ceasefire and dangerous situation. This created a powerful trigger, escalating to a tipping point towards resumption of the civil war, genocide, and the region-wide destabilization that has devastated the Great Lakes region since then.

Paul Kagame has to be immediately brought to account for this crime and its consequences. First, there is absolutely nothing honorable or heroic in reaching an agreement for peace with a partner, and then stabbing him in the back. Kagame and Habyarimana did not meet on the battlefield on April 6, 1994. If they had, and one of them or both had died, it would have been tragic, but understandable, as a product of the logic of war. President Habyarimana was returning from a peace summit, and by killing him, Kagame demonstrated the highest form of treachery. Second, Kagame, a Tutsi himself, callously gambled away the lives of innocent Tutsi and moderate Hutu who perished in the genocide. While the killing of President Habyarimana, a Hutu, was not a direct cause of the genocide, it provided a powerful motivation and trigger to those who organized mobilized and executed the genocide against Tutsi and Hutu moderates. Third, by killing President Habyarimana, Kagame permanently derailed the already fragile Arusha peace process in a dangerous pursuit of absolute power in Rwanda. Kagame feared the letter and spirit of the Arusha Peace Agreement. As the subsequent turn of events has now shown, Kagame does not believe in the unity of Rwandans, democracy, respect of human rights and other fundamental freedoms, the rule of law, power sharing, integrated and accountable security institutions with a national character, and resolving the problem of refugees once and for all. This is what the Arusha Peace Agreement was all about. That is what is lacking in Rwanda today. Last, but not least, Kagame's and RPF's false narrative, denials, and deceptions have led to partial justice in Rwanda and at the International Criminal Tribunal for Rwanda, thereby undermining prospects for justice for all Rwandan people, reconciliation and healing. The international community has, knowingly or unknowingly, become an accomplice in Kagame's systematic and shameful game of deception.

I was never party to the conspiracy to commit this heinous crime. In fact, I first heard about it on BBC around 1:00 am on April 7,

1994, while I was in Kampala where I had been attending the Pan African Movement conference.

I believe the majority of members of RPF and RPA civilians and combatants, like me, were not party to this murderous conspiracy that was hatched and organized by Paul Kagame and executed on his orders. Nevertheless, I was a Secretary General of the RPF, and a Major in the rebel army, RPA. It is in this regard, within the context of collective responsibility, and a spirit of truth-telling in search of forgiveness and healing, that I would like to say I am deeply sorry about this loss of life, and to ask for forgiveness from the families of Juvenal Habyarimana, Cyprien Ntaryamira, Deogratias Nsabimana, Elie Sagatwa, Thaddee Bagaragaza, Emmanuel Akingeneye, Bernard Ciza, Cyriaque Simbizi, Jacky Heraud, Jean-Pierre Minaberry, and Jean-Michel Perrine. I also ask for forgiveness from all Rwandan people, in the hope that we must unanimously and categorically reject murder, treachery, lies and conspiracy as political weapons, eradicate impunity once and for all, and work together to build a culture of truth-telling, forgiveness, healing, and the rule of law. I ask for forgiveness from the people of Burundi and France whose leaders and citizens were killed in this crime. Above all, I ask for forgiveness from God for having lied and concealed evil for too long.

In freely telling the truth before God and the Rwandan people, I fully understand the risk I have undertaken, given Paul Kagame's legendary vindictiveness and unquenchable thirst for spilling the blood of Rwandans. It is a shared risk that Rwandans bear daily in their quest for freedom and justice for all. Neither power and fame, nor gold and silver, are the motivation for me in these matters of death that have defined our nation for too long. Truth cannot wait for tomorrow, because the Rwandan nation is very sick and divided, and cannot rebuild and heal on lies. All Rwandans urgently need truth today. Our individual and collective search for truth will set us free.

When we are free, we can freely forgive each other and begin to live fully and heal at last.

Dr. Theogene Rudasingwa
Former: RPF Secretary General, Ambassador of Rwanda to the United States, and Chief of Staff for President Paul Kagame.
E-mail: ngombwa@gmail.com;
Washington, DC. October 1, 2011

15

MAKING SENSE OUT OF KAGAME'S UNINTELLIGENT
RESHUFFLES (*July, 2011*)

During the Cold War, there was a proliferation of experts who
made a living in making sense out of the Soviet complex power
structures. Of particular significance was the May Day Parade,
when signals could be picked about the rise and fall of
personalities by just looking at who sat near the General Secretary
of the Party, or with whom the Secretary exchanged smiles. Such
is the state of Kagame's secretive and deadly police state. We have
to attempt to decode Kagame's latest reshuffle in his spying, and
increasingly criminal, network.

Just to remind the reader that Kagame runs both formal and
informal networks that compete as well as conflict. One thing they
have in common is that their loyalty is to one man, Kagame, and to
an overall mission that he alone defines. In Kagame's Rwanda, the
mission is to do all things necessary to maintain his absolute power
even if this means killing opponents, spying on each other,
eavesdropping on RPF's functionaries, senior members of the
executive, the judiciary and the legislature. Principal among the
formal security organs are the National Intelligence and Security
Service (NISS), till the reshuffle headed by Dr. Emmanuel

Ndahiro, now fallen from grace, and the notorious Directorate of Military Intelligence (DMI), previously headed by Col. Dan Munyuza, now to head the external wing of the NISS. Kagame personally staffs these organs with incompetent sycophants who he can use at will in his criminal schemes at home and abroad. The informal network, however, is even more deadly. The likes of Maj. Gen. Jack Nziza who has a formal job as Permanent Secretary, Ministry of Defence, has, at least until now, the ears of both the President and the First Lady, in running the bigger part of the informal network.

In looking at who comes in and whom goes out in these organizations, one can tell the deepening crisis in Kagame's camp:

1.General Karenzi Karake, now to head NISS. Smart and independent-minded, traits that have landed him into trouble with Kagame, a President who is yet to feel secure in his job even after so many years running the show. Kagame hates KK (as commonly known) with passion. The general has been in and out of jail, once during RPF's pre-1994 period, and recently when he was humiliated and put and house arrest. He is no stranger to the Intel world. The posting is not necessarily one without risk, nor one that shows a dramatic rise in Kagame's trust in KK. Lt. General Gatsinzi, a marginalised Hutu, and Lt. General

Kayumba Nyamwasa, a Tutsi previously held the NISS position, before he was banished to India as Ambassador.

2. Brigadier General Rutatina, now to head DMI. Rutatina, an incompetent sycophant par excellence, is being rewarded by Kagame because he has been outspoken in hurling insults to opposition leaders, especially to Gen Kayumba and his three other colleagues who co-authored Rwanda Briefing. With Dan Munyuza and Jack Nziza (if he is not punished for the leaked YouTube videos in the Kayumba assassination attempt) will lead the effort in entrenching Kagame's repressive machinery at home and abroad. Kagame has a very low opinion of this officer, and were it not that an enemy of my enemy is my friend; Rutatina would be much further from the halls of power.

4.Col.Dan Munyuza, now to head NISS's External Intelligence. Col. Munyuza's fortunes have risen after a death threat and jail term from Kagame. Now Kagame's Poisoner-In-Chief, Munyuza is a man with very limited understanding of the world in which he is supposed to exercise the craft of intelligence. His best bet is to please his master by hunting down Rwandan refugees and poisoning them when and where he can. Kagame could never have trusted Munyuza in the rank and file of an army that he takes to be his personal estate.

5.Col. Tom Byabagamba, now to head counter-terrorism unit at the Ministry of Defence and Rwanda Defence Forces! The most important development with Col. Byabagamba is that for the first time, he is no longer the key element in Kagame's personal security, and the Presidential Guard, the privileged elite army within the Rwandan army whose first and last mission is to protect Kagame and his family. His fortunes, and those of his family, have been on the decline. David Himbara, once Kagame's Principal Private Secretary, has taken refuge in South Africa. His wife, Mary Baine, lost her job at Kagame's cash cow, Rwanda Revenue Authority. Her sister-in-law Rosemary Museminari, abruptly and disgracefully lost her job as Minister of Foreign Affairs. In the intrigue that reigns high at Kagame's court, the young officer lost out in the contest that is increasingly shaped by other upcoming First Family favorites.

6.Dr. Emmanuel Ndahiro, previously the boss at NISS, is the greatest loser in Kagame's latest moves on the Rwandan chessboard. Dr. Ndahiro, until he became the head of the NISS, had never held any formal office. He rose to influence by being Kagame's personal doctor and errand boy. Nothing Dr. Ndahiro cherishes more than being known as the guy who has the ear of his chief. And boy, he has used it conveniently and relentlessly against friends and colleagues, as he supplied endless lists of enemies to a boss who demands them with the zeal of a paranoid schizophrenic. As Kagame's errand boy, he is privy to many, many, illicit transactions (eg. the executive jets deals), military purchases, and criminal operations abroad (e.g. the Kayumba Nyamwasa's attempted assassination). Dr. Ndahiro is tied to Kagame, ad infinitum. How the drama plays out can only be speculated.

Note that all of these gentlemen are all RPF and Tutsi. The Minister of Defence, Lt. Gen. James Kabarebe is a Tutsi. So is the Chief of Defence Forces, Lt. Charles Kayonga; the Army Chief of Staff, Gen. Caesar Kayizari; and Permanent Secretary, Ministry of Defence, the notorious Maj. Gen. Jack Nziza. The writing is on the wall! Where else on this planet earth is a ruler who is so insensitive to the nature of his country's challenges to the point of being ridiculous? If one says the Hutu are particularly being marginalised, with grave implications, would this be treason, punishable with death, jail, or exile? If one says this small clique of Kagame's Tutsi kitchen cabinet is not representative of all Tutsi, and therefore endangers their future, is that betrayal?

Kagame is losing. The national democratic struggle for freedom is gathering momentum after Brussels, London, Chicago and London again. Rwandans are slowly but surely overcoming fear that is the main weapon Kagame uses against them. The world that Kagame has taken for granted as allies is slowly waking up to the realities of Rwanda and the danger that he poses to the Rwandan people, Rwanda's neighbors in the Great Lakes region, and the international community. Under pressure, he reshuffles, reshuffles and reshuffles. Unintelligent reshuffles will not save him. Nor will killing Rwandan people, taking away their resources for personal use, and absolute dictatorship intimidate them into silence and inaction. On the contrary, these reshuffles, and occasional cosmetic changes, are the sign that Rwandan people are winning in the struggle to co-create a free, united, peaceful, and democratic Rwanda in which the rule of law and shared prosperity are the rule, not the exception.

16

KAGAME'S DIPLOMACY IS BROKEN: HOW TO RE-INVENT IT (*August, 2011*)

A couple of weeks ago President Museveni of Uganda, his wife and child visited Rwanda, and was warmly received by his counterpart, President Kagame. A few weeks before then President Kagame's wife had visited the Museveni family in Uganda. During the four-day state visit, Museveni and Kagame put on their best appearances, said the right things, participated in community work, dined together and told Rwandans and Ugandans that all is good. Shortly after the Rwanda visit, President Museveni visited South Africa for talks with President Jacob Zuma. A few weeks from now, on September 12, 2011, President Kagame will be a guest to President Sarkozy in Paris, France.

Speculators, spectators, analysts, and citizens of Rwanda and Uganda are asking themselves, what is going on here? Are Museveni and Kagame now determined to put behind them the recent deep mistrust between them and build new friendly relationship? What are Museveni's interests in Kagame and Rwanda? What are Kagame's interests in Museveni and Uganda? What role, if any, does Kagame and Museveni need, want, or expect South Africa to play in the Rwanda-Uganda drama?

Even more difficult questions can be asked about Sarkozy and Kagame. One wonders what President Sarkozy expects to gain from courting Kagame. In the same way, it requires a stretch of imagination to understand what Kagame's calculations and expectations are in his new venture in France. Unlike the Kagame-Museveni relationship, where one can point to a time when there was some friendship, there is no love lost between Kagame and France. How can we understand this unfolding drama?

In this mix, introduce the role of the United States and the United Kingdom, the two countries that Kagame considers so crucial to the survival of his regime to the extent that it is what he cares about more than anything else, and certainly not the aspirations of the Rwandan citizens.

Consider the following ten maxims of diplomacy:

First, diplomacy is about projecting and protecting a nation's national interests, stupid!

Second, idealism may occasionally be mentioned as the driver of diplomacy (freedom, human rights, democracy, etc.), but realism about what is possible is what really drives a nation's diplomacy

Third, nations (especially big powers) use hard power (gunboats) or soft power (money, culture, public diplomacy, etc.) to get what they want

Fourth, there are neither permanent friends nor permanent enemies, only permanent interests.

Fifth, a nation's domestic environment (politics, economy, social conditions, culture, etc.) influences how it looks at the outside world, and its diplomatic posture

Sixth, in a country where governance is characterized by the absolute rule of one man, diplomacy is his exclusive prerogative, and he must use it to prolong his rule against the interests of his people and his nation. The so-called national interests are his personal interests; and his personal interests are national interests

Seventh, a nation's neighborhood, comprising of other states with which it collaborates and competes at the same time, influences its diplomatic outlook

Eighth, 21st Century diplomacy is witnessing non-traditional actors, or non-state actors that for good or for worse wield tremendous power and influence (global businesses, armed networks, NGO's, citizen groups, etc.)

Ninth, technology, especially social media, is proving to be a powerful tool in enhancing a nation's diplomacy, just as it can undermine and constrain its diplomacy because citizens in and outside the country have access to it.

Tenth, diplomacy is often about appearances and perceptions rather than reality.

Through the lens of these maxims, one can see that Kagame is an embattled ruler who is taking diplomatic gambles in the hope of delaying his eventual downfall. He is an absolute ruler at home who imprisons and kills political opponents at home and abroad. He is accused by the United Nations Human Rights Commission of serious human rights abuses, war crimes, crimes against humanity, and even possibly acts of genocide. He has kept hundreds of thousands of Rwandans as refugees, whom he wants repatriated by force to bring them under the sphere of control like the 11 million citizens who are his hostages. He has taken a belligerent posture towards Rwanda's neighbors. He has gone to war twice in the Democratic Republic of Congo. His army fought Museveni's army in Kisangani, DRC. He keeps a proxy force in eastern Congo to destabilize and plunder that country. The leaders of DRC and Burundi are perpetually fearful for their own personal lives, and for their shaky governments that Kagame directly or indirectly undermines. In France, Kagame has a dossier that hangs above his neck like the Sword of Damocles. In the past when anything about the death of President Habyarimana in a plane crash in 1994 has been raised by French judges, Kagame has thrown tantrums, swore that he does not give a damn, banished the French language in Rwandan schools, thrown out a French ambassador and broken diplomatic ties with France. With South Africa, diplomatic relationships are at their lowest due to the attempted assassination of General Kayumba Nyamwasa in 2010, by Kagame's security agents. More than ever, Kagame's regime is feeling the heat of the resistance that is gaining momentum at home and abroad.

When Museveni went to Rwanda, he was aware of all that, and aware that Kagame is predictably unreliable. Museveni is also aware that Kagame is a very vicious and vindictive man who does not rest or spare any resources to kill his opponents (including Heads of State!). He is aware that Rwanda's army, the RDF, has been organised on the basis that the enemy to be fought is anybody and everybody who is not with Kagame (principally his Rwandan political opponents, but also includes Museveni's UPDF and DRC). Museveni would have been aware that if the worst came to the worst, Kagame could precipitate a Uganda-Rwanda war to conceal his internal troubles. While for sure Kagame does not hesitate to support those who are opposed to Museveni, he only assumes that Museveni supports those opposed to him (Kagame). Museveni does not support Rwanda's opposition. Museveni would also have been aware that he and Kagame have mutual friends-the USA and the UK-who are not happy that the two African allies wash their dirty linen in public. Finally, Museveni talking points would have included that fact that Rwanda's small economy is Uganda's major export market.

One wonders what was achieved by the Museveni visit, apart from the appearances and perceptions. Such visits and bilateral talks have taken place before, followed by temporary calm, later to be followed by the same path of mistrust and acrimony. If Museveni came out of the visit assured that he is personally safe, that a border war is not imminent between the two countries, that Kagame will not support Museveni's opponents, that goods and services would continue being sold in Rwanda, and finally that the relationship between the two Presidents is on the road to rehabilitation in the eyes of the USA and UK, it would have been a great success. Kagame's main interest is that Museveni will not support Rwanda pro-democracy forces. The presence of George Mitchell, UK Minister for International Development, a man who adores Kagame like an idol, was present during the Museveni visit, checkbook in hand, just in case his services were needed by the duo as a sweetener.

It is on the South African front that things remain shaky. It is possible that Museveni may have been asked by Kagame to intercede on his behalf and ask Jacob Zuma to help in extraditing Gen. Kayumba Nyamwasa and Col. Patrick Karegeya back to Rwanda, or at least relocate them. It is possible that Museveni could have been asked to convey Kagame's wishes to President Zuma to do everything possible to end the Kayumba attempted assassination court case, because of the involvement of Rwanda state security agents.

The Franco-Rwanda relations (or be specific, France-RPF or France-Kagame relations), it is important to note first; France lost its influence in Rwanda in 1994. The political, defence and intelligence establishments that were supportive of the Habyarimana regime have received tremendous bashing from Kagame and his RPF. France has been accused by Kigali for supporting a genocidal regime. A cloud of guilt and uneasiness hangs on the conscience of France. Within the defence and intelligence community in France, there is no love lost with Kagame, whatever he does. Loss of influence in Rwanda, a gain for the Anglo-Americans, cannot be taken with a smile. President Sarkozy may visit Rwanda, and invite Kagame to Paris, thanks to the efforts of France's former Foreign Minister, Bernard Kouchner, and those of Kagame's lobbyist former UK Prime Minister, Tony Blair and his business network in France. There are still many ghosts in the France-Rwanda relationships that need to be pacified and tamed. Second, Kagame has a serious problem in France. This is the problem of French judges investigating the President Habyarimana plane crash and the indictments that point fingers to Kagame himself. Kagame hopes it will melt away, and that intimidation, denials and deceptions could nip the matter in the bud. What is the bargain between Sarkozy and Kagame? Can Sarkozy prevail over an independent judiciary to doctor the findings of the investigations in Kagame's favor? This is doubtful. If Sarkozy was to appear even minimally supportive of Kagame's policies, against the wishes of his Foreign Minister, Alain Juppe, and the judges, what would Kagame give in return? Rwanda's small agrarian economy of 11 million does not provide a worthwhile promise. Or that Kagame would now "pardon" the French and give them back the influence they had before 1994? Could it be that Kagame would promise that he would add France to the short list of interests (mainly US and UK) on whose behalf he acts as a gatekeeper to the Democratic Republic of Congo? Can he be a servant of more than two competing masters without hurting one and favoring others? Both Kagame and Sarkozy are taking diplomatic gambles that at the best are of little benefit, and at their worst counter-productive.

This brings us to the question of US and UK interests in Rwanda. From the tragedy of 1994, there might be an element of altruism, wanting to help the victims of genocide and war. The altruistic argument becomes unsustainable given the fact that the altruism becomes one-sided, favoring some victims and ignoring others. Tutsis were victims of genocide. Hutus have been victims of Kagame's RPF regime's war crimes, crimes against humanity, and even possible acts of genocide in Rwanda and DRC, according to a United Nations mapping Report. The US and UK, and the international community have not shown any concern to bring to accountability those who committed these crimes. There is also the problem of the guilt conscience of the international community. Since you did nothing to prevent or stop the 1994 genocide, Kagame and RPF charge, then shut up and do as we say! Kagame and RPF have used this weapon effectively for the last 17 years. The third factor is Kagame's role as a policeman who keeps the gates to a region that is both fragile but promising to US and UK security and economic interests. The Democratic Republic of Congo is of particular interest. The fourth factor is that together with others in this region, especially Museveni of Uganda and Zenawi of Ethiopia, Kagame is seen by some circles in London and Washington DC as crucial, if not critical, to US and UK security interests in central, eastern and horn of Africa. Ethiopia and Rwanda have the largest contingents in Darfur, Sudan. Uganda's army is deployed in Somalia and before it Ethiopia was instrumental in previous operations. The fifth factor is probably ideological. Kagame "accepted" to make Rwanda join President Bush's "coalition of the willing" against Sadam Hussein in Iraq. Recently, as the drums of war intensified against Libya's Gaddafi,

Kagame was probably the only Africa leader who wrote in favor of NATO actions. Finally, of late Rwanda's so-called "socio-economic miracle" has become a show case in development circles, particularly in the UK Department of International Development (DFID). Kagame might be a dictator, so the argument goes, but his state is efficient and effective in utilising western aid. Short of success in many parts of the world, there are those in London and DC who want to push for Rwanda as a successful model of economic development. They forget that it is not the first time Rwanda is seen as "developing", that this development leaves out the majority of the Rwandan people, that it is not sustainable because it is too dependent on aid, and that development without very basic freedoms is sham and short-lived. In summary, the US and UK give a lot to Kagame, which keeps his regime alive. In return, Kagame gives them what they want and need. In the process, it is the interests of the Rwandan people, which are sacrificed.

Kagame's diplomacy is irreparably broken. Here is how to re-invent it.

The Rwanda National Congress, together with other pro-democracy voices of Rwanda is laying the foundations for a new, people-centered diplomacy for Rwanda. The primary point of departure is Rwanda's interests. Between Rwanda's and other nations' interests, mutually beneficial outcomes can be negotiated. Rwandans cannot afford any longer to be the losers all the time.

In the short term, the diplomacy of Rwanda's pro-democracy voices is centered on persuading African countries especially Rwanda's neighbors, and the whole international community (especially the USA and UK) to support the following:

(a) Calling for the immediate and unconditional release of all political prisoners

(b) Demanding an end to persecution (including arbitrary arrests and detentions, torture, involuntary disappearances and extra-judicial killings) of government opponents and critics and their relatives

(c) An end to the practice of channeling the development assistance that the is provided to Rwanda through budget support

(d) Conditioning the development assistance that is provided to Rwanda government on political reforms, including opening up political space

(e) Using regional and United Nations human rights mechanisms to ensure that President Kagame and his security officials are held accountable for gross human rights violations that are committed against innocent citizens

(f) Ensuring the protection of all Rwandan refugees and resisting attempts by the Government of Rwanda to force the UNHCR to apply the cessation clause by end of 2011; and,

(g) Encouraging the government of Rwanda to agree to a comprehensive and unconditional dialogue with the opposition on ways for resolving the political impasse engulfing Rwanda

In the medium to long term, RNC together with other Rwanda's pro-democracy forces expect respect for Rwanda's national interests, and diplomacy based on the following:

1. Stop and prevent violent conflict, including genocide and grave human rights violations that Rwanda's people have periodically suffered and that have historically extended to citizens – men, women, and children – of neighboring states;

2. Eradicate a culture of impunity for human rights violations;

3. Create a conducive and progressive environment for inclusive social and economic development for all the people of Rwanda;

4. Establish, nurture and institutionalize democratic governance, particularly the rule of law in all its aspects;

5. Establish independent, non-partisan, professional civil service and security institutions;

6. Build a stable society that promotes and protects equality, embraces and celebrates diversity, and fosters inclusion in all aspects of national life;

7. Promote individual, community and national reconciliation and healing;

8. Promote harmonious relations, reconciliation and mutually-beneficial collaboration with the peoples and governments of neighboring states;

9. Resolve the chronic problem of Rwandan refugees;

10. Nurture a culture of tolerance to diverse ideas, freedom of discussion, and debate of critical issues.

The writing is on the wall for President Kagame. In private as he has watched the events in Tunisia, Egypt, Libya and other places unfold; he might deceive himself that his diplomatic gambles, friendship with people in high places and protection by powerful nations will sustain him. He should be reminded that Egypt, Tunisia and Libya were immeasurably much bigger economies, had bigger armies, and certainly were much higher stakes with respect to western geo-strategic, security and economic interests. Only two years ago, there was a stampede as western politicians and businesses scrambled to call on Gaddafi in his desert tent. He was received in western capitals, including Paris, where Kagame will dine with who is who in France. Today, Libya is in turmoil and Gaddafi's days seem to be numbered. Kagame has committed far worse crimes than Gaddafi's, but he is still received with pomp and circumstance.

Today Kagame has friends. Tomorrow his friends might turn out to be his worst enemies. When that happens, or even before, there will always be Rwandans ready to build a new diplomacy towards a new Rwanda that will be a united, democratic, and prosperous nation inhabited by free citizens with harmonious and safe communities who will live together in peace, dignity and mutual respect, regardless of class, ethnicity, language, region, origin or other differences, within a democracy governed according to universal principles of human rights and the rule of law. To the international community, and especially to France, USA and the UK, we say: there is absolutely nothing that Kagame gives or promises that Rwandans cannot give you with better value, if it is right and fair. It is time to choose. No need to wait for a Gaddafi moment, with the death and destruction that comes with it

17

"I DON'T GIVE A DAMN!" (*June, 2011*)

Addressing journalists on his return from the fateful trip to

Chicago, President Kagame was in his usual angry, denial and

deception mode. About demonstrations in Chicago, he said there

were only 20 Rwandans waving the picture of his assassinated

predecessor, President Habyarimana, and the old Rwanda flag.

About shocking revelations that he personally was involved in

Gen. Kayumba Nyamwasa's assassination attempt in South Africa

one year ago, he was characteristically agitated, evasive and

cynical and said it was fabricated by amateurs.

The worst direct insults were reserved for Human Rights Watch

and Amnesty International because of their reporting on the grave

and deteriorating human rights situation in Rwanda, and indirectly

to London Police for warning Rwandans in the UK that the

Government of Rwanda was planning to kill them. He called their

reports "nonsense" and "pathetic". He said he does not know them,

and that he has never asked help from them. And, in his trademark

phrase whenever asked about deaths of Rwandans he has to

account for, he charged, "I don't give a damn!" What a role model

to children?! In conclusion, he also said he had become wiser in

the last seventeen years.

Of late President Kagame has become obsessed with the word "values" or "agaciro" (in Kinyarwanda). What an irony that the man whose actions and words show extreme disregard for the most important of all human values-respect for the sanctity of human life-would have the guts to make it his losing campaign theme. Killing innocent citizens, lying, and insulting truth-tellers and whistle-blowers have never been indicators of wisdom. They are the telltale signs of an absurd and tragic figure, attempting to drag a whole nation and its 11 million people to his own inevitable demise.

Beware Rwandans, let Kagame sink alone!

18

BEYOND THE BIG STICK, CHEQUEBOOK AND GUNBOATS
(*June, 2013*)

An Open Memo to President Barack Obama on the Eve of his Trip
to Africa

Your Excellency,

Shortly, you and your family will board Air Force One and head to
Africa, on a journey that will take you to Senegal, Tanzania and
South Africa. During your first term in the White House you
visited Ghana, where you made the famous 'Africa does not need
strong men, it needs strong institutions' speech, and Egypt, before
it became engulfed in the Arab spring revolutionary fervor.

In a sense, you return to the same huge planet (30.22 million sq.
km) comprising of 54 countries and a combined diverse population
of 1.033 billion. It is the same Africa considered by many, as the
cradle of humankind, and one that has lured fortune hunters, be
they slave traders, colonialists, vicious spies during the Cold War,
or modern day states and corporate types in search of business and
natural resources.

Being a good student of history, you are familiar with Africa's
contending narratives. Our continent falls perfectly within the

'glass half-full or half-empty' analogy. Of late, many among
Africa's ruling elite and the international community have
amplified their voices; selling the idea that Africa is on the
ascendancy, destined to become a powerhouse within the next few
decades. To them, the glass is half-full. On the other hand, there
are those who point to Africa's sore spots and open wounds;
poverty, HIV/AIDS, illiteracy, poor infrastructure, poor
governance, human rights abuses, violent conflicts and terrorism,
failed or failing states, and environmental degradation. To these
folks, Africa is your typical half-empty glass.

Between these two extremes of optimism and pessimism lies the
true condition of the African people, which you are invited to seek
to learn about, first and foremost. This is the world that, on behalf
of the most powerful nation on planet earth, you can help
overcome human suffering and shape the hopeful place of peace
and prosperity that Africa desires to become. History will,
unfortunately, remind you that Africa is not particularly a place to
secure a permanent positive legacy among great American
Presidents.

Yet, for you, Mr. President, the stakes could not be higher, simply
because of the initial high expectations that greeted your
Presidency. Africans expected, and remain hopeful, albeit with

reduced expectation, that the first African-American U.S. President with a very recent African ancestry will do much more than his predecessors.

I am convinced beyond doubt that you have pondered this matter over and over again. How will Africans remember you? How can this Africa visit create value for African and the American people? Here is some open advice, assuming it gets past the gatekeepers at the White House and State Department to get to you:

First, be aware that the United States carries historical and current negative baggage in Africa in terms of its allies in Africa. Even as the Cold War recedes in the minds of the older generation, there is a discrepancy between what successive U.S administrations claim to be a values-driven foreign policy (freedom, democracy, human rights) and guilt by association with some of Africa's most notorious dictators, as long as they serve 'U.S. interests'. Without being contrite, you may need to assure African people that the U.S will do no harm, and slowly disengage from the company of corrupt big men who usurp institutions and abuse people's fundamental rights.

Second, the U.S should engage pro-democracy and modernizing voices among the political forces, civil society, women and youth organizations, academic institutions and communities. Out of these

will emerge the new leaders and managers of Africa, just as an
enabling environment allowed you to emerge as the U.S. President
in 2008. The U.S. embassies in Africa should take the lead in this
engagement. Historically, when these embassies are not
compromised by the local ruling elite, or too involved on behalf of
narrow U.S. security and economic interests, are often irrelevant
because they are far removed from the ordinary lives of Africans.
Instead of being a beachhead from which to deploy the whole of
U.S. government and international power to make sustainable
impact on the lives of Africans, and hence win their hearts and
minds, the embassy can become a theater for pitched battles among
various departments and agencies. New and innovative marching
orders to U.S embassies in Africa are long overdue, in terms of
who they serve and to what ends.

Third, be aware of revolutionary pressures that are building up
within Africa's youth bulge, the hundreds of millions of
unemployed, unemployable, and often-uneducated young men and
women. Extremist ideologies and religious fanatics find fertile
ground among the marginalized. Of late, if your embassies and
intelligence analysts are telling you (or know) the truth, there is a
growing anti-American, anti-West, sentiment that is both
concealed and open. The publicized economic growth in Africa in
recent years, largely from natural resources, hardly reaches the
poor. The international community, United States included, does

not significantly help willing countries to invest in higher
education or small and medium enterprises to create jobs and a
motive to hope for the future among the jobless youth. You may
wish to announce two bold and inter-related initiatives for higher
education (especially in science, technology, innovation and
entrepreneurship) and, small and medium enterprises (SMEs), and
mobilize the whole international community (UN, World Bank,
EU, AU, Regional Trading Blocs, Bilateral organizations and
Philanthropy) towards this goal. The resources could be pooled
together regionally to motivate cross-border co-operation.

Fourth, invest in holistic women and children health at the
community level, with HIV/AIDS, TB and Malaria integrated at
this level, with a bias towards prevention. This year alone, over
four million under-fives will die in Africa due to preventable
conditions. It is estimated that in the same period more than a
quarter of a million mothers in Africa will die during delivery.
Africa's future is bleak without putting women and children at the
centre of the development and foreign policy agenda. Mrs.
Michelle Obama and your daughters will be disheartened to learn
about this unacceptable high death toll among Africa's women and
children.

Fifth, to help end and prevent conflicts in Africa, encourage,
champion and support negotiations, accommodation and consensus

building, In particular, in the Great Lakes region of Africa, support Tanzania and the SADC initiative, which calls on Rwanda, DRC and Uganda to hold talks with their armed and political opposition. Fortunately, your visit takes place a time when the United States is poised to talk to the Taliban. One makes peace with enemies. As the world holds its breath during the recovery of Nelson Mandela, a legendary icon with a large African heart, bring it to the attention of Africa's big men in the Great Lakes region that Africa is much better off when Africans talk to their fellow Africans, in the interest of African people.

Sixth, reign on your national security team. The hawks among them will insist that there is a red threat (China) looming over Africa, which must be contained or neutralized. Furthermore, these hawks argue, U.S. security and economic interests should take precedence over anything else, even if this means baby-sitting some of Africa's most dangerous big men. The idealists in your team would love to re-invent Africa in a U.S. image. Both pathways are not only undesirable but also unachievable and dangerous. Africa needs China, the United States and the rest of the world for mutual advantage. U.S, China and the rest of the world need Africa for the same reasons. The premium is on healthy competition and co-operation.

Seventh, be aware of the rising tide of two world religions, Islam

and Christianity, on the African continent. From the north to the
south, east to the west, the ordinary people in every African
country have generally lived together peacefully for centuries, as
your 2009 speech in Cairo articulated. Both Islam and Christianity
have largely been forces for good, and together they make Africa
what it is and stronger. Everything must be done to prevent
anything that would put Muslims and Christians on a collision
path, re-enacting the jihads and inquisitions of the past.
Engagement and accommodation, rather than prejudice and
isolation, should be the American way of navigating the ultra-
sensitive terrain of faith, in order to harness the most synergies for
U.S. and Africa's interests.

To summarize, Mr. President, as you travel around Africa, use
your big stick, chequebook and the threat of America's gunboats as
arrows in your quiver, to be used wisely. If you have to promise a
cheque, let it be to support Africa's youth in education, small and
medium enterprises, and women and children health. Disengage
the U.S. from the cozy relationship with Africa's big men, and
engage to help create conditions for authentic pro-democracy
African leaders to emerge. Tame the ambition and temptation for
the U.S. to over-promise and over-reach, in search for enemies to
contain or destroy, or in the hope of creating an Africa that is a
replica of the United States. Promote negotiated and peaceful
settlements, and reach out to the Mosques and Churches to

promote inter-faith dialogue and co-operation.

Ultimately, it is out of the challenges and opportunities of today that Africans themselves must curve out the peaceful and prosperous Africa of tomorrow.

I wish you, your family, and the U.S. delegation a safe trip as you rediscover the magic of Africa.

Highest considerations.

19

CARROTS AND STICKS: FROM APPEASEMENT TO
COEARCIVE DIPLOMACY IN THE GREAT LAKES REGION
OF AFRICA (*May, 2013*)

In their current shuttle diplomacy in the Great Lakes region, Jim

Yong Kim, President of the World Bank, and Ban Ki-moon,
Secretary-General of the United Nations, have spoken on the need
for Rwanda and the Democratic Republic of Congo (DRC) to
commit to peace in exchange for $ 1 billion in aid. In Kigali,
Rwanda, both Presidents lamented the 1994 genocide, expressed
guilt for international failure, and, as usual, praised President
Kagame and called upon him to contribute to peace in the region.

Last year, due to pressure from the international community,
President Paul Kagame reluctantly agreed to have his creation and
proxy, M23, to withdraw from Goma. As a result of this
international pressure, President Kabila was influenced, also
reluctantly, to talk to M23, to listen to its 'grievances.' Admittedly,
the problems of eastern DRC are largely a Congolese problem of
internal weaknesses. However, since 1994, Rwanda has exported
its own internal political and human rights crisis to DRC. Although
the current problem in the eastern DRC has a Congolese
component, the M23 saga is Rwanda's deliberate creation. You

cannot solve, once and for all, the 'M23 problem' without dealing with Rwanda's own political crisis, and re-evaluating the West's hitherto unquestioning support to President Kagame. Short of new and innovative ways in the thinking process, policy, and action to underpin diplomatic, political and aid-related initiatives, current peace initiatives will be a temporary and futile measure.

The Great Lakes region is amidst a period of high risk and escalation in Rwanda and the Great Lakes region. Within Rwanda, we are probably two to three years to major events, which could escalate into a full civil war. The political space has become completely closed, with moderate voices dead, in jail or in exile. The regime has become ever more illegitimate, intransigent, and aggressive. Power is vested in the hands of President Kagame and his wife, and a few Tutsi military officers who run both the formal and informal government. President Kagame and his top military officers have ceaselessly turned to the DRC for personal economic gain, the latest venture being the M23, itself with high potential to escalate into a full civil war that could easily turn regional and ugly. They are the same officers that are at the heart of the so-called M23 rebellion and the horrendous crimes, which were described in the UN Mapping Report of 2010 and other previous reports. Many people in Rwanda, DRC, Great Lakes region, Africa and the International Community are asking about the endgame in the current crisis in DRC.

Even with the deployment of the 3,000-strong international
brigade, in addition to the 20,000-strong UN peacekeeping force
with US $ 1.5 billion annual budget, sooner than later the costly,
redundant and scandal-prone UN peacekeepers in DRC will cut
down their losses and close down what has become an
embarrassingly ineffectual operation. The international
community, especially the United States, United Kingdom, France,
Belgium, United Nations, and the World Bank face a mountain of
credibility gaps that are both historical and current. African people
in the Great Lakes region do not trust that these players are honest
and impartial brokers. Nor do they trust their own governments,
whose governing elite are largely the source of the cyclical crises
in Rwanda, Burundi, DRC, and Uganda.

Here are some ideas for an all-inclusive, society-wide, regional,
Africa-led, approach for responding to the immediate humanitarian
crisis. In the medium and long term such an approach should help
in de-escalating the violent conflict, stopping the impunity that
underlies mass atrocity and other gross human rights abuses,
promoting inclusive political and economic arrangements, building
strong institutions that enhance the rule of law, co-operation for
national and regional security, and building resilient communities
for shared peace, and sustainable prosperity.

First, immediately initiate a coordinated two-track peace process for Rwanda and the Democratic Republic of Congo. The two-track peace process should be co-facilitated by South Africa and Tanzania, under the auspices of the African Union. The permanent members of the United Nations Security Council (United States, United Kingdom, Russia, France and China), and the European Union should be engaged observers to the peace processes.

Second, call a spade a spade. The contact group, comprising of the co-facilitators and the observers, should be brutally honest to all the regional players involved in the problem. The international community should halt the policy of appeasement born out of the failures of 1994. The contact group collectively has substantive leverage and wisdom to bring to the table. The members of the contact group should seek to understand the current power dynamics in Rwanda and the DRC, appreciate the consequences of maintaining the status quo and inaction, and consider the threats and opportunities with respect to international peace and security.

Third, adopt a people-centered approach. The contact group should directly engage Rwandans and Congolese struggling for fundamental freedoms and justice. A timid international community that will not care for African people, and will only look at the each country and the region through the eyes of rulers is a recipe for cyclical conflict and disaster. The thousands of civil, community and political groups that are calling for change in these countries are, like their own societies, imperfect, but still they are indispensable stakeholders. The international community must support efforts that promote genuine dialogue, reconciliation and healing within Rwanda and DRC. It is not good value for money when billions are spent in development projects when many in Rwanda and the DRC feel they are marginalized within and outside their countries.

Fourth, seek and promote accountability to end impunity, with an end goal of promoting restoration rather than retribution. However, Africans and the rest of the international community must make sure that those who have committed, and continue to commit, horrendous human rights abuses, war crimes, crimes against humanity and genocide are held accountable. Economic efficiency, though desirable, is not the only factor in human development as founding and policy documents of the United Nations and the World Bank testify. Without basic rights and human dignity, the so-called economic development is both sham and unsustainable.

Fifth, the contact group should urgently convene a Great Lakes Peoples Conference (GLPC) to consider a 'Great Lakes Peoples Compact' to motivate the tens of millions of the unemployed, youth, and women who are both victims and tools of predatory state and non-state actors. The conference should invite governments, community and civic groups, business, academics, political opposition, multilateral and bilateral organizations to promote buy-in in the peace process.

Throwing money and hastily organized peace deals among the principal spoilers at a protracted and complex problem, without redressing its root causes, is a recipe for another failure and disaster. The challenge to resist repression and war, and build viable communities and institutions is primarily an African affair. However, the international community should have an interest in supporting Africa's efforts before it is too late. A window of opportunity does exist, but it is closing fast. We must act innovatively, and together, now.

20

THE UNITED STATES OF AMERICA: INDISPENSABLE NATION OF EMPIRE IN PERIL? (*October, 2013*)

On September 9, 2013, the United Nations published its second World Happiness Report, but the top ten happiest nations in the world did not include the United States of America. A week later Forbes magazine published a list of the richest 400 Americans. On September 16, a lone gunman shot and killed twelve innocent people at a Washington Navy Yard. On Saturday afternoon, September 21, 2013, the peace enjoyed by Kenyans was shattered by a vicious terrorist attack by Al-Shabab, a Somali "non-state actor", in a standoff that left at least 68 dead and 175 injured.

On September 25, the United Nations General Assembly convened in New York, in United States, for the usual annual ritual of speech making, shopping, and compiling reports. Among the numerous reports of the United Nations was one by the Intergovernmental Panel on Climate Change on the environmental state of our planet earth. The expectations from such an event were scaled so low so that the world should celebrate that the United States called off a military attack against Syria for using chemical weapons against its people. We are supposed to be jubilant because of fifteen minutes of a telephone conversation between U.S. President Barack Obama and the Iranian President Hassan Rouhani.

On October 1, the United States Federal Government was shut down over budgetary disagreements between the ruling political classes. On October 3, the United States Government imposed sanctions on five countries (Rwanda, Syria, Burma, Central African Republic and Sudan) for use of children soldiers in deadly conflicts. On the same day, the White House announced that U.S. President Barack Obama had cancelled his trip to Asia due to the U.S. Government shutdown.

On October 4, in Lampedusa, Italy, a shipwreck left over 111 Africans dead. The Africans were heading to Europe in search of a better life.

We may ask ourselves what these seemingly isolated or 'chance' events have in common: a lone gunman, a terrorist non-state actor like Al-Shabab, rogue state actors that send their children to war instead of schools, Africans dying on high seas, a super power that shuts itself down and an American president who cancels a trip to the world his country is supposed to shape, and a global body like the United Nations which is both taken serious and ridiculed for its impotence.

I am an African from Rwanda who lives in Washington DC.

Logically, I am the least qualified to comment authoritatively on the business of these United States. However, like millions before me, I am grateful that I was welcomed as a life-long nomadic refugee into this nation. My family is comprised of American citizens. I must say I am fascinated and intrigued by the bold human experiment that these United States represent. This nation has endowed itself and human civilization with giants in all walks of life. It has, at the same time, received much from the world. It has created abundance far beyond what human beings could possibly imagine.

On deeper reflection, one gets a very unflattering image of this nation. It is angry, grumpy, indulgent, violent, fearful, divided, distracted, in debt, addicted to power and material stuff, and in a self-inflicted siege. Like the Biblical prodigal son, it has squandered its wealth and now, as America looks at herself in the mirror, she does not like what she sees. Millions of Americans are hurting and uncertain of the future. Hundreds of millions worldwide would have hoped for inspiration because the United States is supposed to be the place where dreams are fulfilled.

Yet, how can it engage in self-destruction and hope to lead itself and the rest of the world? How will the United States deter the likes of Al-Shabab and Al Qaeda when here in America it is fine to buy automatic weapons from a shop next door and kill innocent children, men and women? How will the United States be taken serious by Syria, Iran, Rwanda, Korea and Sudan when it threatens to use force and sanctions, and its friends and foes discover it is a fractured superpower, torn asunder by petty quarrels, greed and selfishness? How will America claim to fight poverty and disease abroad, when it is divided over something as basic as health care and job opportunities for all Americans?

How can this "American problem" be fixed?
America must find a balance between the quest for individualism and the needs for community and society. Individualism in America has been pushed to the extreme. Human beings do not solely exist to always be "me, myself and I," where, like a fool, one thinks, "let me drink, eat, and be merry for tomorrow I die." All Americans should benefit from common pools of knowledge and material wealth. Nor should Americans accept a society and communities that impose unnecessary restrictions and burdens on the individual's quest for responsible fulfillment.

The idea of capitalism, the source of entrepreneurship, innovation and economic growth must be managed wisely in the interest of all stakeholders of society. Unfettered capitalism that produces a minority of winners and a majority of losers is very unstable. Like communism that promised utopia but ended up with chained societies, the American brand of macho capitalism is inherently unstable and unsustainable. Health, education and job opportunities for Americans are not privileges but indispensable conditions for America's existence.

The critics of the Obama administration say the government has been transformed into an overbearing welfare state. The Obama people say, in crisis, a responsible government must extend help to those who find themselves at the bottom of the socio-economic pyramid. In normal times, government must invest in common pools that citizens must draw from: health, education, infrastructure, security, institutions, laws, etc. This is a healthy centuries-long debate that must continue. There is, however, a middle ground occupied by the top performers in the UN World Happiness Report 2013 (Norway, Denmark, Sweden...). Maybe America, too used to being a teacher, might be a humble student as well and learn from the world beyond itself.

American society must come to terms with violence at home. The image of America from the margins is that of a superpower always itching for a fight abroad, because its citizens love violent movies, guns, and shooting people. This is a mistaken view in reference to the majority of American people. Why do American citizens need guns? Some say because there are bad people out there! Yes, but the evolution of the state historically has entailed a tough bargain that we should consider: if the state can monopolize the means of violence, then we can all draw from the common pool of security. At the end of the day, no amount of individual weaponry could provide 100% of one's required security. History simply shows how weapons have generally fallen in the wrong hands and American society continues to pay a heavy price in innocent lives lost.

Americans, especially the politicians, must learn to tame the appetite for demonizing each other, which, driven to the extreme, has led to the shutting down of the government, and in worst case scenario, can lead to rapture within the whole of American society. Coming from Rwanda, a nation that has suffered for too long from hatred fueled by political competition and ethnic fears, I detect a very pernicious and poisonous atmosphere here in Washington DC. The political class seems to be busy shuffling chairs, throwing stones at each other on the deck of the ship, America, while it is on the verge of sinking. There are undertones of race, ideology and sheer opportunism in the saga. Be careful America, you too are not immune to the ultimate consequences of extreme hatreds. Democracy is messy, but it must be managed so that it does not gravitate towards chaos and destruction.

A strong, secure and prosperous America needs a strong, secure and a prosperous world around it. When Europe, Asia, Africa and Latin America are strong, America has a lot to gain. The pictures of Africans dying on high seas, pirates on the Indian Ocean, terrorists striking at will, conflicts fueled by dictators and marginalized populations; HIV-AIDS, widespread global joblessness, global warming and poverty are not the conducive atmosphere for America to be secure and prosperous.

The United States is often called upon to act or not to act. The United States must engage. Often, America does not engage. It rules. The too familiar image is one of the trigger-happy nation, with drones, aircraft careers and soldiers rumbling on like Rambo of the Hollywood movies. Yet America has tremendous soft-power resources that can shape for good the 21st Century. This requires deploying its hard power multilaterally with others, and when done unilaterally, with exceptional humility and responsibility. An atrophied United Nations and regional organizations that are conveniently ignored or manipulated by the United States, does little good to the United States and the peoples of the world.

Most importantly, the United States must regain balance and rediscover its moral purpose. For a long time, America has packaged itself as the city on a hill, leading by example, the nation whose ideals and practices are so powerful because they are so endearingly smart and fair. If democracy leads to shut down of governments because, in simple terms, some politicians feel sections of the populations should not be allowed to have health care, should that model be emulated, ignored, or avoided?

Americans, this is your teachable moment. The poignant words of Jeremiah, an ancient Jewish prophet, are right and fitting for the moment: "seek the peace and prosperity of the city to which I have carried you......pray to God for it, because if it prospers, you too will prosper." A broken America will ultimately break all Americans, and with it, the world. A strong and fair America, with a moral purpose, will lift all American individuals, families, states, the nation and the world.

21

SHAPING THE FUTURE WHILE LEARNING FROM THE PAST: A RESPONSE TO KAGAME AND MUSEVENI (*April, 2014*)

I read in today's *Wall Street Journal* an opinion written by President Paul Kagame with a catchy title, "Reflecting on Rwanda's Past-While Looking at the Future", and President Yoweri Museveni's speech in Kigali , Rwanda.

Their opinions indeed demonstrate the defining characteristics of the Presidents of Rwanda and Uganda: an alchemy of militaristic threats, myths, deceptions, and denials.

Paul Kagame: *After a genocide, historical clarity is an inescapable duty. Behind the words "Never Again," there is a story whose truth must be told in full, no matter how uncomfortable.*

Fact: It is not only after a genocide, but generally in every human undertaking as important as nation-building, where historical clarity is an indispensable obligation. The truth must be told in full, including by those who hold on to power through illegitimate arrangements, however uncomfortable the truth may be to them.

The people who carried out genocide, war crimes, crimes against humanity and continuing human rights abuses were, and still are, Rwandans. And those Rwandans include Paul Kagame who provided a trigger for the genocide (the shooting down of President Habyarimana's plane), and his leading role in the war crimes, crimes against humanity, and even possible acts of genocide against Hutu in the Democratic Republic of Congo. That is the truth.to be told.

Paul Kagame: *We do so with humility of as a nation that nearly destroyed itself...*

Fact: Rwanda has been on a slow but steady journey of self-destruction for several decades, interrupted by turning points when national tragedy becomes inevitable. Such was the case in 1959, and 1994.

Credible nation-builders must turn to history to draw sufficient wisdom to avoid the mistakes of the past. That is where humility becomes a vital asset. Paul Kagame, in words and deeds, lacks the humility to see the striking similarities of his regime to the weaknesses in the pre-colonial order that exposed it to its capture by colonial powers; the vulnerabilities of the hybrid monarchy-colonial order that made the 1959 Hutu revolution inevitable and legitimate; the decline of the Kayibanda regime that led to the rise of the Habyarimana regime in 1973; the internal crisis of the

123

Habyarimana regime that led to its eventual collapse; and, notably, the current abhorrent conditions in the Kagame regime that make violent revolution almost inevitable. The writing is on the wall, but Kagame lacks the humility to recognize that his regime's days are numbered.

Paul Kagame: *All genocides begin with an ideology—a system of ideas that says: This group of people here, they are less than human and they deserve to be exterminated.*

Fact: All genocides, war crimes, crimes against humanity and all other forms of injustice are mainly committed by dictatorships. Dictatorships have an outlook, a narrative, and an ideology. While Kagame's RPF was founded with a nationalist and democratic vision, its practice has delivered it into the hands of a brutal dictator whose ideology is power at any price, thriving on imposing a blanket guilt on Hutu, and fear on the Tutsi.

Germans, Belgians or the French did not invent Tutsi and Hutu. Yes, their own interests helped to politicize the identities. This was not entirely a bad thing, because for centuries power was in the hands of small minority that reproduced Tutsi kings and the system that nourished them. The politicization of identities had its down side, but it did produce possibility of change within its womb.

The Catholic Church nurtured the Tutsi kings and later worked against them, throwing their weight behind the popular 1959 Hutu revolution, which eventually degenerated into narrow Hutu cliques. Belgium, the United Nations, France, and the Catholic Church progressively missed the opportunity to be agents for promoting positive change towards national unity, democratization and the rule of law, but they should not be accused of having taught Rwandans to look at each other as less than human, and to have participated in genocide.

Certainly, the Holy Bible does not teach that. It teaches love, without which Rwandans are prone to inflict trauma on each other, when encouraged and facilitated by brutal dictatorships.

More than fifty years after Rwanda's independence from Belgium, Rwanda's elite must stop being crybabies, conveniently denouncing foreigners every time their systems are crumbling due to their own misrule. Should Rwandans in future denounce the British and the Americans, allies of the Kagame regime since 1994, as perpetrators of the crimes that Paul Kagame and his Tutsi clique have committed, and continue to commit? Should the Anglican Church, now allied to the state, be responsible for the crimes that Kagame and his regime commit against Rwandans? Certainly, no!

Yes, the US and British Governments, and the Christian church, like the Belgians and the French before them, are missing the opportunity to help Rwandans towards freedom, democratization, and national unity, the rule of law, healing and reconciliation. History will judge them harshly unless they change course,

Paul Kagame: *In Rwanda, we are relying on universal human values, which include our culture and traditions, to find modern solutions to the unique challenges we faced in terms of justice and reconciliation following the genocide.*

Fact: Rwanda's traditional culture is centered on the African principle of *Ubuntu*. Embedded in this are the universal human values of love, truth, justice, self-respect, and respect for others. To the extent that these enhance our freedom, and freedom expands our choices, we can claim to be modernizing. There cannot be reconciliation and healing without forgiveness. Forgiveness presupposes the freedom to tell the truth. Kagame and RPF have sacrificed freedom, truth and forgiveness for political expediency in order to maintain power at any price.

Paul Kagame: *Early on, we made three fundamental choices that guide us to this day. First, we chose to stay together. Second, we chose to be accountable. Third, we chose to think big. We may make mistakes....We own up and learn and move forward.*

Fact: Staying together, accountability and thinking big are NOT the distinguishing characteristics of the Kagame regime. The country is more polarized than ever before on inter-ethnic (Hutu-Tutsi) and intra-ethnic (within the Tutsi and Hutu communities). In fact, the rationale of the annual Remembrance Day is to remind Rwandans and the world that Tutsi are the victims and Hutu the perpetrators of genocide.

If Kagame's regime was accountable, it would let the whole truth be told, and the perpetrators of crimes against Hutu in Rwanda and the Democratic Republic of Congo be known and brought to justice. It would let Rwandans know who carried out the assassination of Seth Sendashonga, Theoneste Lizinde, Patrick Karegeya, Andrew Rwisereka, Augustin Cyiza, Jean Leonard Rugambagye, Charles Ingabire, Colonel Patrick Karegeya, the multiple assassination attempts on General Kayumba Nyamwasa, and many others. If accountability was its goal, it would explain to Rwandans and the world why Victoire Ingabire, Bernard Ntaganda, Deo Mushayidi and many others are languishing in jail as political prisoners.

Accountability is about free speech, free association, open political space, independent media, and active civil society, all of which do not exist in Rwanda today.

Thinking big is not simply and solely about skyscrapers, clean streets of Kigali, economic growth and doctored statistics on social indicators. Previous governments registered positive developments in all the sectors, which successive regimes can build on.

On both accounts, Kagame's score is a failure.

Accountability is about telling your party, RPF, the government and the Rwandan people how much money Kagame pockets from Crystal Ventures, the Horizon Group, public finances, and the plunder of natural resources from the Democratic Republic of Congo.

The greatest challenge to Rwanda is how to first, redress the dynamics of power that hitherto have been hijacked by ethnic-based elites, and, second, how to build national institutions that can help foster national unity, freedom, democracy, healing and reconciliation

If you cannot keep Rwandans together, and you cannot account to them, then the claim of thinking big is simply hollow.

Paul Kagame: *Our approach is as radical and unprecedented as the situation we faced. The insistence on finding our own way sometimes comes with a price.*

Fact: What is radical and unprecedented about Kagame's reign is not its inclusiveness, innovation or far-sightedness. Its belligerence in the Great Lakes region and its exceptional brutality in dealing with political opponents are radical and unprecedented. This comes at a price indeed. Kagame's regime has made enemies at different times with the Democratic Republic of Congo, Uganda, Angola, Zimbabwe, Namibia, Tanzania, South Africa, Belgium, France, not to mention the majority of individuals and organizations that it has made a habit of antagonizing.

Yoweri Museveni: *We all can witness the economic growth in Rwanda and its stabilization. As a veteran patriot of this area, I would like to warn those who hobnob with the genocidaires to know that they will have to contend with the patriotic forces that defeated the traitors with their external backers when they were still much weaker. We are now much stronger in every sense of the word (politically, militarily, socially and economically). The People of Rwanda should know that they can always count on the People of Uganda. Uganda is steadfast in the support for African emancipation.*

Fact: Well, some of us Rwandans have generally desisted from commenting on Ugandan matters, despite the fact that we are more schooled on Uganda than Yoweri Museveni is on Rwanda. We are not impressed at all by his ignorance of, or his insensitivity to, the plight of the Rwandan people, and the facts of contemporary Rwanda. His refrain of economic growth and stabilization is a familiar recital of the standard narrative of Kagame and his international supporters, who choose to ignore the fact that the majority of the population is poor.

His claim of being "a veteran patriot of this area" is an attempt to hang on to his now-extinct pan Africanist credentials.

Museveni and Kagame have now become the Mobutus of this era, being a source of plunder, war making and destabilization in the Great Lakes region and the Horn of Africa. Reactionary veterans, yes. Patriots, no!

Museveni and Kagame are more isolated in Africa and internationally than ever before. Their regimes are weak politically because they lack popular support. Economically, they are dependent on Western benefactors, who are increasingly embarrassed by the association. Socially, they run polarizing regimes that sap the social capital of their societies.

Museveni the political scientist has probably forgotten that military strength is but one component of overall national strength. Without a strong political, economic, social and professional base, the Ugandan and Rwandan militaries are just a pack of cards, distinguished in intimidating citizens for a while, but unable to withstand the pressure when populations mobilize, get organized and are well led.

Museveni has been battling his Ugandan foes without defeating them for as long as he has been President. Now, the Pan Africanist of yesterday has to swallow his pride and depend on US Special Forces. In 2001 he had to beg Clare Short, then British Secretary for International Development, to give him resources to build Uganda's military, ironically to fight the Rwandan army whose leaders (Kagame and RPF) he described as ideologically bankrupt. Kagame has fought armed Rwandans in the DRC for almost 20 years without defeating them.

The Ugandan and Rwandan military and security establishments have been progressively degraded, their officer corps retrenched, to the extent that the remaining majority are silent while the rest owe their loyalties not to the nations and their peoples, but to Museveni and Kagame. The cross-border trio that presides over the criminalized network that abducts and kills Rwandans, and terrorizes Ugandans, include Brigadier Muhoozi Kainerugaba (Museveni's son), General Kale Kayihura (Inspector General of Police, Uganda), and Major General Jack Nziza (Kale Kayihura's relative, and Kagame's hangman who runs his assassination network). Both Nziza and Kale are Bafumbira from Kisoro, Uganda.

Paul Kagame: *To prevent genocide, it is not enough to remember the past. We must also remember the future.*

Fact: To prevent genocide, it is critical to have the humility to remember and learn from the past, so that we may not repeat the mistakes of the past. Kagame and RPF have advanced and progressive amnesia, hoping that forgetting recent history will save them forever. Unfortunately, history is very unforgiving. Remembering the past so as to shape the future, like "Never Again", should not be an empty slogan or cliché. People have to build together, and trust is the glue that holds everything together. Rwanda's trust account is now in red.

Here is a ten-point genocide prevention compact for Rwanda:

1.Stop and prevent violent conflict, grave human rights violations that Rwanda's people have periodically suffered and that have historically extended to citizens – men, women, and children – of neighboring states;
2. Eradicate a culture of impunity for human rights violations;
3. Create a conducive and progressive environment for inclusive social and economic development for all the people of Rwanda;
4. Establish, nurture and institutionalize democratic governance, particularly the rule of law in all its aspects;
5. Establish independent, non-partisan, professional civil service and security institutions;

6. Build a stable society that promotes and protects equality, embraces and celebrates diversity, and fosters inclusion in all aspects of national life;

7. Promote individual, community and national reconciliation and healing;

8. Promote harmonious relations, reconciliation and mutually-beneficial collaboration with the peoples and governments of neighboring states;

9. Resolve the chronic problem of Rwandan refugees; and,

10. Nurture a culture of tolerance to diverse ideas, freedom of discussion, and debate of critical issues.

Paul Kagame: *Les faits sont têtus—facts are stubborn, and no country is powerful enough, even when it thinks it is, to change the facts.*

Fact: Messrs Kagame and Museveni, here is my message to both of you. Facts are stubborn, and no dictator is powerful enough, even when he thinks he is, to change the facts. The wind of change is blowing. You can choose to ignore it, but you cannot stop it. For both of you the writing is on the wall. You have betrayed the nationalist, Pan-African, and democratic cause. You have been weighed on scales and found wanting. The days of your regimes are numbered.

We are not easily intimidated by Museveni's sabre rattling, and his threats that he will fight alongside Kagame against nationalist and democratic forces in Rwanda. When that happens, it will be their turn to be defeated together, decisively, justly, and swiftly.

Their opportunistic marriage of convenience cannot stand the patriotic unity of Rwandans, Ugandans and other Africans.

It makes our work a lot easier to know our friends and foes.

22

KAGAME'S CHARM OFFENSIVE IN AMERICAN
UNIVERSITIES (*April, 2014*)

Paul Kagame has been touring top American universities giving

speeches deceiving unsuspecting students and uncaring top brass at

these academic institutions about what he calls accomplishments of

his reign peace, human rights, democracy, development, etc. This

is vintage Kagame: he has the entire Rwandan population under

lock and key, assassinates and imprisons dissenting voices, and

then goes to the land of his benefactors to taunt the West as if to

say, "I do what I want, you can go to hell!"

Other than his love of million dollar luxury trips, (money that

ends in his private pockets because he rents the private jets bought

on public money to the Rwandan state) and expensive $20k a

night hotel, and an opportunity to visit his children studying here in

the USA. Kagame seems to be thrilled to receive honorary

doctorates and rub shoulders with academics. For a man who never

stepped in a university out of indiscipline, and not lack of

intelligence, has he discovered that universities are useful centers

of learning, contributing to human progress?

Universities have historically been places where intellectual

freedom, openness, and innovation have been nurtured. It is then ironical that Kagame the enemy of freedom and openness in Rwanda would be welcomed to Harvard, Tufts, MIT, Brandeis, and Stanford to extol the same values that he lacks and fights. He should be grateful to Tony Blair, Bill Clinton, Michael Porter, Rick Warren, Michael Fairbanks and other hired mercenaries whose greased hands can return favors that enable dictator Kagame to hobnob with academics who do not care about the plight of Africans.

Of late Kagame has not been received with fervor at U.S. State Department and the White House. He must be secretly lamenting that. Universities provide an alternative opportunity to be around here, and to continue his campaign of deceptions and denials. On this particular trip, he seems to be indirectly telling his strongest supporter, the United States, that he will change the constitution, and run for as long as he wants, and nobody will stop him.

Kagame's threats must be taken seriously. He has killed and waged wars with impunity.

He is fond of saying privately that the West and the so-called international community lacks the interest and will to stop him from doing what he wants.

He is right in this regard but wrong in another sense. Rwandans have the interest and will to stop and reverse the effects of his murderous madness.

When that happens, and Kagame survives the coming change in Rwanda, Tufts, Harvard, Brandeis, MIT and Stanford should perhaps crown him with a tenured professorship of dictatorship. After all, he has stolen enough money to offer generous endowments to these otherwise prestigious but heavily commercialized institutions.

Shame on you Tufts, Harvard, MIT, Brandeis, and Stanford!

23

AFRICA'S BETRAYAL BY AFRICAN LEADERS (*May, 2014*)

Africa's, and international's, elite have just concluded the African Development Bank's 50th anniversary celebrations and annual meeting under the theme: "The Next 50 Years: The Africa We Want". Over 3,500 delegates, Seven African Heads of State, the Governor of the Central Bank of China, and U.S Deputy Secretary of Treasury are among the dignitaries to grace the occasion. The guests and the host were in an upbeat and hopeful mode, predicting that the next five decades will be far better than the preceding ones.

There are enough grounds to celebrate some of Africa's political, economic and social achievements since 1957, when Ghana blazed the trail to become the first to gain political independence from British colonial rule. Africa can now boast of a total population that exceeds one billion, 54 sovereign states, and a rich endowment of natural resources. There is every reason for Africa to celebrate its shining moments, the founding fathers of the post-colonial order who shaped them, and the African people who make them happen.

Beneath the confident calm, Africa is on edge and the participants in Kigali were aware. After five decades of political independence, thousands of reports on human development, tons of advice from mainly Western consultants, and trillions of aid money, the condition of the majority of African people remains precarious. Africa remains the continent of peasants, and increasingly of urbanized populations living on the margins of squalid slums bursting at the seams.

Africa's silent emergency comes in the form of pernicious killers in the form of poverty, hunger, disease, illiteracy, and unemployment. These preventable conditions claim millions of African lives every year because they target Africa's heart and soul: children, women, the elderly and peasants. Though the statistics do not capture the full and often intangible extent of human suffering and lost opportunities, they are nevertheless shocking. According to UNICEF, annually there are 3.2 million under-five deaths in Sub=Saharan Africa from preventable conditions; Africa is the most dangerous place to have a baby in the whole world (800 women die every day during pregnancy and child delivery, and half of these deaths are in sub-Saharan Africa). Over 11 million Africans under the age of 25 enter the labor market every year, only to swell the ranks of the unemployed.

Africa's loud emergencies are exemplified by the hundreds of missing Nigerian girls still in their captors' hands, another terrorist attack in Kenya last Friday, civil war in Central African Republic and Southern Sudan, continuing conflict in the Democratic Republic of Congo, a failed state in Somalia, Rwanda and Burundi sliding into civil war, Uganda's long-running battles with Joseph Kony; standoff in Egypt, uneasy peace in Libya, to cite a few examples. A report *"Africa's Missing Billions"*, by the international charity, Oxfam, "showed that between 1990 and 2007 the cost of armed violence and conflict to Africa was $300 billion – approximately the same as the aid money that flowed into the continent during that time. Losses continue at around $18 billion a year. Conflict shrinks the economies of affected African countries by at least 15% a year"

Hence, as the elite in Kigali concludes the summitry and deliberations, there is the other part of Africa that is on fire, dying, burning silently and occasionally bursting into deadly conflict and tragedies.

Unable to find hope, jobs, inspiration and the reason to live, Africa's youth have become the easy victims of war-lords, rabble rousers, demagogues and modern day slave traders. Africa's youth, which should be the continent's present and future, have been turned into pirates, terrorists, rebel child soldiers, and sex slaves. Dreading the conditions in their own countries, they take dangerous voyages into uncertain worlds, and they perish on high seas as they did last October, 2013, in Lampedusa, Italy; or, in the case of a 15-year old Somali boy who stowed away in an airplane last month from San Jose, California, bound for Hawaii, in search of his mother in a refugee camp in Ethiopia.

If Nigeria (population approximately 174 million, largest oil producer in Africa, and annual defense spending of 2.3 $ U.S.) cannot rescue its own young girls from Boko Haram, and Uganda cannot defeat a three-decade old menace from Joseph Kony and his Lord's Resistance Army, will a handful of U.S. Marines and aircrafts save them?

Africa has a crisis of leadership. Many of Africa's rulers have, by and large, betrayed African people for too long.

If this is the diagnosis, what is the treatment plan?

First, Africa's ruling elite must admit that they are mostly to blame for Africa's problems. They must stop the opportunistic habit of depending on the West's help (East as well during the Cold War), and denouncing the same benefactor when Africa's self-inflicted wounds become too obvious. Unless there is a change of mindset, African elite will continue to act like a herd, yesterday behind the West or East, today the West or China, and tomorrow, God knows who. Africa must follow its conscience and its people's interests.

Second, African leaders must recognize that the interests of African people are sovereign and therefore, a first priority. Of these interests, nothing is more important than the right to life, security, health, education and livelihoods. It is in this context that Africa must spend less on armies and armaments, because African countries do not generally fight each other. Africa's armies fight their own people, and record shows that they generally do an exceedingly poor job at that. African leaders must stop denying fundamental human rights to their population. Freedom and equal opportunity will unleash entrepreneurial energy that has historically transformed other societies. They must invest in education, health, rural and urban areas where the majority of poor Africans live, and small and medium enterprises. In all these areas, women and youth should be given priority.

Third, Africa leaders must have a clear and robust strategy to exit from being the dependent patient, in and out of rehab or intensive care of aid. Africa's natural wealth must beget value. Africa's export of natural resources, national revenues, foreign investments and aid money must be deployed and recycled into developing the capital, knowledge and skills to create value-added products and services. This is the trajectory of wealth creation that the rich aid-givers of today follow. Africa is not an exception.

Fourth, African leaders must prevent and cure the recurrent epidemics of self-inflicted conflicts. The current fire-fighting demonstrated in international peacekeeping, drones, and ad hoc arrangements for U.S and Western armies to intervene in Africa can be temporary relief but are not sufficient to ensure lasting security and peace. Conflicts within African countries remain matters of unresolved problems because of the cut-throat competition for power among the elite. It is a life-and-death struggle to capture state power, and in turn use it to access and hoard resources, and/ or dispense a victor's justice to the losers. The winner takes it all, and often the losers must accept their losses, or otherwise organize for the next round of bloody conflict since the status quo rarely yields peacefully. The antidote to this is to democratize and enlarge the circle of people's participation in governance, strengthen the rule of law, and nurture a culture of dialogue, power-sharing, and peaceful resolution of conflicts.

Last, but not least, African rulers must heed the wisdom from all cultures of the world. Human progress is not solely about building material abundance and registering GDP growth, important as they are for human survival. Creative imagination, innovation, science, technology and entrepreneurship proceed from man's quest to improve his lot. To do this, he/she discovers that co-operation is both a pre-condition for survival, and an opportunity to demonstrate what Bantu-speaking peoples of Africa call *Ubuntu* (or, human-ness). Africans must learn from their own achievements and flaws, and those of other societies, to nurture the wellbeing and resilience of individuals, families, communities and nations.

A mind rich on *Ubuntu* peels away clan, tribe, gender, race, class, religion, and nation identities to see the brother and sister in the other. Such a mind is not quick to kill and plunder. It does not commit genocide or easily go to war. It is a mind that shares and weeps when others suffer. It is a mind that sees dialogue, respect of

143

others, and humility as strengths. It is a mind that is happy because it fosters happiness in others.

In a stampede to become like the West, and of late, like China, Africa's ruling elite have lost their African-ness, and yet they get frustrated when they cannot exactly emulate the West's and China's ingenuity.

African leaders must change their own mindsets; put women and children at the center of all national and continental endeavors; create an enabling environment for growth of institutions, freedom and the rule of law; champion Made-in-Africa value-added products and services for consumption and exchange; prevent and cure violent conflicts; and, above all, embrace *Ubuntu* as a central organizing philosophy in African societies.

African societies must liberate themselves from chaos, suffering, and dependency.

African leaders must redeem themselves from scorn, shame and condemnation before it is too late.

Africa, be and heal yourself!

24

DO NO HARM: SEVEN PATHWAYS TO FIX BROKEN U.S. POLICIES IN AFRICA (*May, 2014*)

Open Letter to U.S. Secretary of State, John Kerry

Dear Secretary Kerry,

You have been on a tour of Africa that took you to some of Africa's troubled hot spots. In Southern Sudan civil war rages. In the Democratic Republic of Congo, decades of mis-rule, and vicious predatory proxy wars from Rwanda and Uganda, have left behind 6 million people dead and a country that is in shambles. As you tour the continent, you are well aware that Somalia and Central African Republic are burning. Just two days ago terror struck again in Kenya. As you embarked on your journey, 300 innocent young girls were abducted in Nigeria. The United States has its Special Forces and aircrafts in Uganda to capture or kill Joseph Kony, the notorious warlord. Libya and Egypt are on edge. Rwanda and Burundi in central Africa, epicenters of violent conflict and genocide two decades ago, are poised for civil war.

Being a good student of history, you are familiar with Africa's contending narratives. Our continent falls perfectly within the 'glass half-full or half-empty' analogy. Of late, many among Africa's ruling elite and the international community have amplified their voices; selling the idea that Africa is on the ascendancy, destined to become a powerhouse within the next few decades. To them, the glass is half-full. On the other hand, there are those who point to Africa's sore spots and open wounds; poverty, HIV/AIDS, illiteracy, poor infrastructure, poor governance, human rights abuses, violent conflicts and terrorism, failed or failing states, and environmental degradation. To these folks, Africa is your typical half-empty glass. Between these two extremes of optimism and pessimism lies the true condition   of   the   African   people.

Some US policies towards Africa are broken, counter-productive, and harmful to Africans and Americans in the short, medium and long   term.   Here   are   some   suggestions   to   fix   them.

First, be aware that the US carries historical and current negative baggage in Africa in terms of its allies in Africa. Even as the Cold War recedes in the minds of the older generation, there is a discrepancy between what successive U.S administrations claim to be a values-driven foreign policy (freedom, democracy, human rights) and guilt by association with some of Africa's most notorious dictators, as long as they serve 'US interests'. For example, I have always wondered what the United States gets in return for supporting President Paul Kagame of Rwanda and President Yoweri Museveni of Uganda, bloodied dictators responsible for horrendous human rights abuses that fuel deadly conflict in the Great Lakes and Horn of Africa. How can the United States be part of a solution when it is part of the problem? In short, the United States first line of action   is   to   do   no   harm.

Second, the U.S should engage pro-democracy and modernizing voices among the political forces, civil society, women and youth organizations, academic institutions and communities. Out of these will emerge the future leaders and managers of Africa. The US embassies in Africa should take the lead in this engagement. Historically, when these embassies have either been compromised by the local ruling elite, or too involved on behalf of narrow US security and economic interests. Either way they are prone to becoming irrelevant because they are far removed from the ordinary lives of Africans. Instead of being a beachhead from which to deploy the whole of US government and international power to make sustainable impact on the lives of Africans by winning their hearts and minds, the embassy often becomes a theater for pitched battles among various departments and agencies. New and innovative marching orders to U.S embassies in Africa are long overdue, in terms   of   who   they   serve   and   to   what   ends.

Third, be aware of revolutionary pressures that are building up within Africa's youth bulge, the hundreds of millions of unemployed, unemployable, and often uneducated young men and women. Extremist ideologies and religious fanatics find fertile ground among the marginalized. Of late, if your embassies and intelligence analysts are telling you (or know) the truth, there is a growing anti-American, anti-West, sentiment that is both concealed and open. The publicized economic growth in Africa in recent years, largely from natural resources, hardly reaches the poor. The international community, United States included, does not significantly help willing countries to invest in higher education or small and medium enterprises to create jobs and a motive to hope for the future among the jobless youth. The United States should take the lead with the international community to co-invest with responsible African governments in higher education (especially in science, technology, innovation and entrepreneurship) and, small and medium enterprises (SMEs), and mobilize the whole international community (UN, World Bank, EU, AU, Regional Trading Blocs, Bilateral organizations and Philanthropy) towards this goal. The resources could be pooled together regionally to motivate cross-border co-operation.

Fourth, invest in holistic women and children health at the community level, with HIV/AIDS, TB and Malaria integrated at this level, with a bias towards prevention and systems strengthening. This year alone, over four million under-fives will die in Africa due to preventable conditions. It is estimated that in the same period more than a quarter of a million mothers in Africa will die during delivery. Africa's future is bleak without putting women and children at the centre of the development and foreign policy agenda.

Fifth, to help end and prevent conflicts in Africa, encourage, champion and support negotiations, accommodation and consensus-building, In particular, in the Great Lakes region and the Horn of Africa, support Tanzania and South Africa in the peacekeeping work they are doing in DRC. Put pressure on the Presidents of Rwanda, Burundi, DRC, and Uganda to have dialogue with their opponents and open political space. Make it absolutely clear that is a high cost to scheming and changing constitutions to perpetuate dictatorship. Withdraw US support to Presidents Museveni and Kagame until they stop their destabilizing military adventures in DRC and South Sudan, and hold them accountable to their war crimes, crimes against humanity, and acts of genocide.

Sixth, reign on your national security team. The hawks among them will insist that there is a red threat (China) looming over Africa, which must be contained or neutralized. Furthermore, these hawks argue, it is US security and economic interests that should take precedence over anything else, even if this means baby-sitting some of Africa's most dangerous big men. The idealists in your team would love to re-invent Africa in a US image. Both pathways are not only undesirable but also unachievable and dangerous. Africa needs China, the United States and the rest of the world for mutual advantage. U.S, China and the rest of the world need Africa for the same reasons. The premium is on healthy competition and co-operation, with the interests of ordinary African people at the center.

Seventh, be aware of the rising tide of two world religions, Islam and Christianity, on the African continent. From the north to the south, east to the west, the ordinary people in every African country have generally lived together peacefully for centuries. Both Islam and Christianity have largely been forces for good, and together they make Africa what it is and stronger. Everything must be done to prevent anything that would put Muslims and Christians on a collision path, re-enacting the jihads and inquisitions of the past. Engagement and accommodation, rather than prejudice and isolation, should be the American way of navigating the ultra-sensitive terrain of faith, in order to harness the most synergies for US and Africa's interests.

To summarize, Mr. Secretary, the US should do no harm. Use your big stick, cheque-book and the threat of America's gunboats as arrows in your quiver, to be used wisely. If you have to promise a cheque, let it be to support Africa's youth in education, small and medium enterprises, and women and children health. Disengage the US from the shameful relationship with Africa's bloody dictators, and engage to help create conditions for authentic pro-democracy African leaders to emerge. Tame the ambition and temptation for the US to over-promise and over-reach, in search for enemies to contain or destroy, or in the hope of creating an Africa that is a replica of the United States. Promote negotiated and peaceful settlements, and reach out to the Mosques and Churches to promote inter-faith dialogue   and   co-operation.

Ultimately, it is out of the challenges and opportunities of today that Africans themselves must curve out the peaceful and prosperous Africa   of   tomorrow.

Highest considerations.

25

RWANDA'S DIPLOMATIC MISSIONS AS STAGING
GROUNDS FOR CRIMINAL ACTIVITIES (*May, 2014*)

Paul Kagame's 20 year reign of terror is characterized by a
distorted and deceptive narrative that: he saved Tutsi from
genocide perpetrated by Hutu; over- reliance on violence and war-
making nationally and regionally; "Tutsi-fication" of the
leadership of the military while eliminating real and potential
competitors; transformation of the ruling RPF into a rubber stamp
to enforce his will while eliminating real or perceived contenders
to power; usurping legislative, executive and judiciary powers;
closure of political space for political parties, civil society,
independent media and intellectual activity; personal control of a
financial empire that is spread across public and private sectors;
and, a mindset of a serial killer and mass murderer who relentlessly
acts with impunity.

It is out of this anti-people, sectarian and anti-democratic domestic
policy that Kagame's dangerous foreign policy is derived,
characterized by belligerence, aggression, war-making and plunder
in the Great Lakes region; blackmail, grand deception and
intimidation that preys on on international guilt from failure to
prevent or stop the 1994 genocide; an anti-African posture
masquerading behind pan-Africanist language; and above all, an

immoral foreign policy, founded on the premise that opponents, whether heads of state or ordinary citizens, must die or be jailed.

The Kagame doctrine is not simply wrong. It is anti-Rwandan, militaristic. deceptive, predatory, belligerent, anti-African and immoral. In short, it is dangerous for Rwanda, the Great Lakes region, Africa and the international community.

This predatory and highly criminalized foreign policy is executed through its embassies abroad: Burundi, Ethiopia, Kenya, South Africa, Sudan, Tanzania, Uganda, Senegal, DRC, Nigeria, Belgium, Germany, The Netherlands, United Kingdom, Sweden, Switzerland, France, Canada, China, India, Japan, USA, United Nations, South Korea, Singapore, Russia, Turkey,and multiple consulates.

Kagame and about a dozen Tutsi military officers, all former refugees in Uganda, preside over this global criminal enterprise to assassinate opponents. Over the last twenty years, agents of the criminalized Rwandan state have struck terror in the Democratic Republic of Congo and Rwanda, killing millions Congolese and Rwandans. His assassins have struck in Kigali, Nairobi, Dar es Salaam,Kampala, Bujumbura, Maputo, Johannesburg, West Africa, Kinshasa, London, Brussels, and Stockholm. Victims of this criminal crusade include Heads of State, opposition politicians, human rights activists, journalists and ordinary Rwandan citizens.

According to Kigali sources, confirmed by a number of foreign security agencies, Kagame is poised for even more daring criminal moves in the heart of the United States, Canada, and the rest of the world, as he intensifies hiring assassins from far-flung areas of eastern Europe and the Middle East.

To do that, he is directly or indirectly enabled by money accumulated from the state treasury, his companies Crystal Ventures and Horizon Group, and aid mainly from generous benefactors like the World Bank, IMF, European Union, United States and United Kingdom governments. He is enabled by the rich and powerful in the West, notably former U.S. President, Bill Clinton, former British Prime Minister Tony Blair, American Pastor Rick Warren, Jewish Rabbi Shmuley Boteach and scores of western consultants making money from Rwanda's, and the region's, open veins. In Africa, his principal backer and co-accused in regional adventures is President Yoweri Museveni of Uganda.

Rwanda's embassies abroad have become the staging grounds for criminal activity. In addition to so-called military attaches and secretaries, officially accredited as diplomats, there are many other agents deployed informally to hunt down, intimidate, divide, corrupt, and assassinate Rwandans. Non-Rwandans critical to Kigali's domestic and foreign policies have occasionally been victims, and will increasingly be targeted according to Kagame's new desperate directives.

Rwandans must get more united, mobilized and organized to stop these murderous schemes once and for all, through a regime change that must allow sustainable societal transformation to take place.

The international community can no longer claim not to know the depth and extent of criminal activities by Kagame's regime. The international community may choose to remain silent, insensitive and frozen in inertia as in the past.

Alternatively, we urge Africans and the rest of the world community to support Rwanda's struggle for freedom, human rights, democracy, justice for all-- genuine unity and reconciliation, healing, peace and prosperity for all Rwandans and the Great Lakes region

26

URGENT CALL TO ALL RWANDANS: UNITE, MOBILIZE
AND ORGANISE FOR A NATIONAL DEMOCRATIC
REVOLUTION!(*May, 2014*)

For almost all of us Rwandans, we know how much suffering we
are undergoing. We are a fearful nation. On every hill we live in
fear, anger, suspicion, and uncertain of the future. We are in jails in
Rwanda. We are in jails in Arusha, and even when are free, we
cannot go back home as free people. We are banished as refugees
in every corner of the world. We are silent for fear of persecution if
we speak. We are targets of assassination in every corner of the
world. We are in the jungles of Congo, fighting endless wars that
consume lives of young Rwandans and Congolese so that a dictator
may survive longer. We are poor, and yet being forced to give
money to the so-called Agaciro Development Fund, to a dictator
who plunders and kills Rwandans. We clap for the dictator, and
while he is away, or secretly in our hearts, we wish him dead. We
are a humiliated lot, living as second-class citizens in the country
that belongs to all of us.

The revolution is ripe, since there is enough injustice and human
suffering among us Rwandans. The harvest is plentiful. However,
the harvesters are few. Nothing important in life is ever cheap. It

takes nine months of pregnancy, painful labor and a whole lifetime to get and raise a useful human being. Revolutions are even more costly. The number one asset for a revolution is commitment. It cost commitment on the part of Rwandan kings to run the show for several centuries. Even the Belgian colonial enterprise was committed to run Rwanda for decades. It cost commitment to bear and deliver the 1959 MDR revolution. It cost commitment on the part of the coup-plotters to deliver the 1973 MRND regime that lasted until 1994. It cost commitment and sacrifice for RPF to wage and win the 1994 war.

How much commitment do Rwandans have to win the current revolution whose core mission is to unite and heal all Rwandans? If you ask Rwandans, they will tell you they want change immediately. A quick and cheap solution, they will tell you. We spend enormous time on the internet and social media trading words among us and with the dangerous regime in Kigali. We are scattered in organizations that are weak enough to be manipulated, intimidated or bought by the regime. Many of us are neither hot nor cold. They have one foot in the revolution and another in the regime that hunts them down. The Hutu are a marginalized lot, but they dream that one day, as if by magic, numbers will do the miracle. The Tutsi, hostages falsely believing that Kagame represents them, are in denial, thinking that monopoly of the army, intelligence, government and money will save the regime forever.

Kagame's regime is at its weakest since 1994, with little legitimacy among Rwandans and increasingly isolated abroad. This is the time to mobilise and organize, and shorten the agony and suffering of the Rwandan people.

We must face and kill these seven demons that consume our commitment to move quickly to end Kagame's brutal regime:

1. **FEAR**: Fear is the most powerful weapon in the hands of Kagame and his clique. The moment Rwandans overcome fear will be the moment the regime crumbles.

2. **PROCRASTINATION**: Rwandans know what to do and how to do it but they are still trapped in believing that it will be done tomorrow. Yet a day spent procrastinating is another day spent in misery. Laziness has never been an asset. You reap results in direct relationship to how much time, resources and effort you have invested in something.

3. **MINDS TRAPPED IN DENIAL AND DECEPTION**: There still among us who believe we can restore the Rwandan kingdom, regimes of the past (MDR-PARMEHUTU, and MRND) or prolong RPF forever. The past is gone, and gone forever. The best we can do is to learn lessons to help us change the present and re-invent, or re-imagine, the future in which we leave behind the shared bad past, and build on the shared positives in our history.

4. **SELFISHNESS & GREED**: The selfish Rwandans. Especially most of us, the elite, tend to think that the world revolves around us and our immediate family. We have become victims of instant gratification, without thinking about the future of our children and grandchildren. Yes, we still have to service the car, the mortgage, summer holiday, and a lifestyle commensurate with our status. We still have to reserve some of our resources to invest in our common future. Or, sadly, we are "bought" for a plate of jobs and money. We are enticed to "come and see" the new "Rwanda flowing with milk and honey". In our own country, we are asked to come and see, like visitors or strangers. Especially among the Hutu, we have become the generation of "come and see." To come and see your property and that if you fall on your knees they will give back to you what belongs to you. What are we teaching our children? That they must bow in submission if you can only give them a job or food? Is that agaciro, our value?

5. **"THEY WILL DO IT FOR US" MENTALITY"**: There is a false belief among us that somebody will do it for us. The Belgians and the French did it for the Hutu, some say. Others say Americans and the British did it for the Tutsi. The truth of the matter is that Belgians, French, Americans and the British look out and fight for their interests. Rwandans must look out for and fight for their interests first and foremost. Nobody else will. To get friends who support your cause, you must show that you deserve their help, you

merit it and you will put it to good use. But you must show that you are in the driver's seat. That no matter what, with or without their help, you will win anyway.

6. **THE "US vs. THEM" MENTALITY**: Rwanda is so precious that very often we want to have it alone without the other. The other is the enemy. The other is the problem. The other is "inyangarwanda", the unpatriotic guys who hate Rwanda. The other killed my people. Who is holy among us to cast the first stone? The kings? MDR-PARMEHUTU? MRND? RPF? Hutu? Tutsi? We cannot re-invent Rwanda's past. It is shared, the good and bad. We can, however, choose to write our future together. We must be bold and courageous to look at each other from each other's standpoint, and see areas where we can stand and build together, brick-by-brick, one day at a time. We must begin where we live and work. We must reach out to the other. I am in the other. The other is in me.

7. **GUILT AND SHAME**. We have wronged each other for too long that the demons of guilt and shame have robbed us of self-esteem. We speak in whispers so that we are not denounced as genocidaires, Interahamwe, revisionists, those who deny genocide, terrorists, etc. On the internet, we write anonymously so that nobody discovers who we really are. I personally know exceptionally intelligent Rwandans who cannot speak out for fear of retribution from Kagame. One told me he could not be on Radio

Itahuka because they (Kagame et al) would connect his organization with FDLR. Incredible! Somebody with a PHD!! We go to places we shouldn't be to buy identity and acceptance. Now there are people in Rwanda who say they have "Tutsi blood" to gain a foothold within the mafia that rules Rwanda. There are Tutsi who, I was told, used to claim they are Hutu during past regimes. We are what we are. Period. We should be very proud of what we are. We did not bargain with God to be what He made of us. We are the proud sons and daughters of the living God. We have all sinned but WE REFUSE to be held in guilt and shame.

When Kagame taunts us with his death squads armed with cannons and bayonets, we should stand squarely in his face, and like teenage boy David to giant Goliath, say: "who is this uncircumcised philistine who defies the armies of the living God?". We are building a powerful army of free Rwandans, armed with peace, truth and unity. The giant shall soon fall. So, Rwandans summon the courage to slay the demons of guilt and shame, "us vs. them" mentality, selfishness and greed, "they will do it for us" mentality, fear, procrastination, denial and deception.

Nurture your commitment. Stand up and go to work. Or else you will die in humiliation and misery, and condemn future generations to a legacy of servitude.

We shall win!

ISBN-13: 978-1499323627

ISBN-10:149932362X